S0-EXB-769

WITHDRAWN

For Reference

Not to be taken from this room

AMERICAN CITIES CHRONOLOGY SERIES

BALTIMORE
A CHRONOLOGICAL & DOCUMENTARY HISTORY

1632 - 1970

Compiled and Edited by
ROBERT I. VEXLER

Series Editor
HOWARD B. FURER

1975
OCEANA PUBLICATIONS, INC.
Dobbs Ferry, New York

Ref
F
189
.B1
V43

Library of Congress Cataloging in Publication Data

Vexler, Robert I
  Baltimore.

  (American cities chronology series)
  Bibliography: p.
  Includes index.
  SUMMARY: A chronology of important events in Baltimore's history and copies of twenty-one pertinent documents.
  1. Baltimore--History--Chronology. 2. Baltimore--History--Sources. [1. Baltimore--History] I. Title.
  F189.B1V43   975.2'6   73-23235
  ISBN 0-379-00602-2

© Copyright 1975 by Oceana Publications, Inc.

All rights reserved. No part of this publication may be reproduced or transmitted in any form or by any means, electronic or mechanical, including photocopy, recording, xerography, or any information storage and retrieval system, without permission in writing from the publisher.

Manufactured in the United States of America

TABLE OF CONTENTS

EDITOR'S FOREWORD. iv

CHRONOLOGY 1
  Colonial Baltimore 1
  Baltimore City 19
  Post-Civil War Era 53
  New Charter - Home Rule 68

DOCUMENTS 87
  Acts Creating Baltimore Town (1729), Jones' Town (1732) and
    Their Merger (1745) 88
  Address of Roman Catholics to George Washington, 1790 94
  Act Creating City of Baltimore, December 31, 1796 96
  Description of Baltimore, 1799 99
  By-Laws for the Government of the Poor, 1826 101
  Recommendations for the Erection of the Baltimore and
    Ohio Railroad, 1827. 104
  Recommendation for a Rail Road from Baltimore to the
    Susquehanna River, 1827 107
  By-Laws of the Board of Trade of Baltimore, 1849 110
  By-Laws of the Baltimore Corn and Flour Exchange,
    January, 1856 114
  Establishment of the Peabody Institute, 1857 117
  Correspondence in Regard to the Burning of Railroad Bridges
    in Baltimore, May 9, 1861 120
  Creation of Enoch Pratt Free Library, 1882-1886 123
  Report of the Charter Commission, January 27, 1898 127
  Annual Message of Mayor Thomas G. Hayes,
    September 17, 1900 129
  Ordinance Regulating Performance of "The Star Spangled
    Banner," July 7, 1916 134
  Baltimore Land and Transportation Proposals, 1919 136
  Baltimore Plan for Postwar Activity, 1943 137
  Arterial Proposal for Baltimore, October 9, 1944 140
  Industrial Planning in Baltimore, November, 1961 142
  Baltimore City Charter, 1964 144

BIBLIOGRAPHY 147
  Primary Sources 147
  Secondary Sources 148
  Articles 151

NAME INDEX 153

EDITOR'S FOREWORD

Baltimore has played a significant role in the development of the United States. It began to develop as one of the important commercial cities but suffered in the early nineteenth century as a result of the building of the Erie Canal. The construction of the Baltimore and Ohio Railroad and other lines, as well as the development of various industries, played a part in its growth and struggle to regain a position of strength throughout the nineteenth century. Baltimore also played an important part in political developments. Its proximity to Washington, as well as the availability of large meeting halls made the city a prime setting for many of the national nominating conventions in pre-Civil War days. Know Nothingism also played a major role in local and state politics for a period of time.

During the twentieth century the two World Wars, changing modes of transportation, and population patterns interfered with and prevented Baltimore from retaining its position as a commercial, social, and economic leader. In the post war period, reconstruction of the center of the city and the wharves was begun as a means of regaining its commercial position.

This research tool is compiled primarily for the student. The importance of political, social, economic, and cultural events have been evaluated in relation to their significance in the development of Baltimore as one of the major cities that has contributed to the growth of America. Every effort has been made to cite the most accurate dates in the Chronology. Various newspapers, documents, letters and chronicles have been consulted to determine exact dates. Later scholarship has been used to verify this information or to change dates when indicated. Students are urged to consult Thomas Griffith's Annals and John Scharf's Chronicles for further details on Baltimore in the eighteenth and nineteenth centuries.

Because the very nature of preparing a chronology of this type precludes the author from using the standard form of historical footnoting, I should like to acknowledge in this editor's foreword the major sources used to compile the bulk of the chronological and factual materials comprising the chronological section of this work. They are as follows: James B. Crooks, Politics and Progress; The Rise of Progressivism in Baltimore, 1895 to 1911; Thomas W. Griffith, Annals of Baltimore; Clayton C. Hall, ed., Baltimore; Its History and Its People; John Thomas Scharf, The Chronicles of Baltimore; and John Thomas Scharf, History of Baltimore City and County, . . .

Robert I. Vexler
Briarcliff College

COLONIAL BALTIMORE

1632   Lord Baltimore was given a charter granting him territory and the government of the province of Maryland. No chapel, church, or place of worship could be established except by his authority.

1659   Baltimore County was established, including not only all of Harford and Carroll counties, but large portions of Anne Arundel, Howard and Frederick counties.

July 28-30. Patents for land in the neighborhood of Baltimore were issued.

1661   Baltimore County Court held its first session at the house of Captain Thomas Howell. Soon after the court house was built on Bush River at Joppa.

February 8. A warrant was issued to the surveyor general to lay out two hundred acres of land for Alexander Mountenay, afterwards called "Mountenay's Neck."

February 24. Charles Gorsuch patented fifty acres of land, later known as Whetstone Point, between the branches of the Patapsco River. At its end stands Fort McHenry. The same land was patented to James Carroll on June 2, 1702, for two shillings rent per year.

July 20. Captains Thomas Howell and Thomas Stockett, and Messrs. Henry Stockett and John Taylor, commissioners of the county, took up patents. The Court was held at the house of Captain Howell, presiding commissioner.

1662   March 2. Abraham Clarke purchased two hundred acres from John Collett and three hundred acres from Robert Gorsuch. Clarke sold all the land to Thomas Montross on March 7.

1668   January 13. Thomas Cole received a warrant for three hundred acres of land, which he soon after revoked and renewed again on June 8.

August 28. Cole's Harbor was surveyed for Thomas Cole, which was patented to him September 4.

1674   Baltimore County's boundary lines were established by proclamation.

1675	Jeremiah Eaton bequeathed to the first Protestant minister who resided in Baltimore County and to his successor, Stokely Manor, containing 550 acres.
1682	Reverend John Yeo, first Church of England clergyman in Baltimore County, arrived from Calvert.
	November 6. An act was passed establishing towns, ports, and places of trade in "Baltimore County on Patapsco near Humphrey's Creek, and in Bush River on the land near the Court House."
1689	August 1. A Protestant revolution occurred in Maryland. Protestants seized the province without bloodshed and put an end to Roman Catholic rule and domination. In the early spring of 1692, Governor Copely arrived as representative of King William and Queen Mary.
1692	June 9. An act was passed establishing the Church of England in the Province.
1696	January 13. One thousand acres of Cole's Harbor was patented; five hundred went to Daniel Carroll and five hundred to Charles Carroll.
1698	February 17. Cole's Harbor was resurveyed and found to contain only 510 acres. It was patented to James Todd as Todd's Range, June 1, 1700 at the annual rent of 10 shillings 2 1/2 pence.
1704	October 3. An act was passed for marking roads. Roads leading to court houses were marked by having three notches on trees on both sides of the roads. Those leading to churches had trees notched with a slit cut down the face of the tree near the ground.
1708	December 17. An act was passed taxing each gallon of rum, wine, brandy and spirits at three pence, as well as twenty shillings per poll for blacks. In addition twenty shillings per poll were charged on Irish servants to prevent an excessive number of Catholics from being imported.
1711	Charles Carroll sold thirty-one acres of his portion of Cole's Harbor with the mill seat to Jonathan Hanson, who erected a mill.

CHRONOLOGY

1712   The assembly passed an act establishing the Baltimore County Court House at Joppa.

1713   November 14. An act was passed assigning the task to the sheriff of each county to establish speedy and safe delivery of letters.

1715   June 13. An act was passed authorizing that court be held four times a year in Baltimore County on the first Tuesday in March, June, August, and November.

1723   October 26. An act was passed establishing fines for blasphemers, swearers, drunkards, and sabbath breakers.

1725   The boundary between Anne Arundel and Baltimore County was established.

1726   Edward Fell, a Quaker, employed Richard Gist to survey Cole's Harbor or Todd's Range, purchased the rights to it from John Gorsuch. The sons of Mr. Carroll prevented the new grant sought by Fell.

1728   October 4. An act was passed to encourage destruction of wolves, crows, and squirrels, by offering either a bounty or a reduction in taxes. In addition three squirrel scalps or crow heads had to be produced annually; one was fined if they were not presented.

1729   July 30. Baltimore was founded two hundred miles from the ocean on a branch of the Patapsco River. Land was to be purchased from Charles and Daniel Carroll.

     August 8. Major Thomas Tolley, William Hamilton, William Buckner, Col. William Hammond, Dr. George Walker, Richard Gist, and Dr. George Buchanan were appointed commissioners to lay off the town of Baltimore. Gist, Hamilton, Buchanan, and Walker agreed on a price for sixty acres with the Carrolls.

1730   June 16. The general assembly passed an act for the construction of a church in Baltimore.

     July 12. Phillip Jones, county surveyor, laid off Baltimore Town.

1742   August 22. John Bayley shipped on the *Elizabeth* under Captain David Frazer four hogsheads of Maryland leaf tobacco to Joseph Adams in London at £9 sterling per ton.

1745 September 28. The assembly passed an act combining Jones' Town and Baltimore into one town.

1747 The shipping interests of Baltimore and its vicinity showed an increase from one vessel a year to seven.

July 11. An act was passed enlarging Baltimore by adding eighteen acres between Jones' Town and Baltimore. The commissioners were authorized to widen the streets with permission of proprietors, to remove nuisances, and to hold two annual fairs on the first Thursdays of May and October.

1748 Messrs. Leonard and Daniel Barnetz from York, Pennsylvania, erected a brewery on the southwest corner of Baltimore and Hanover streets.

1750 The First German Reformed Congregation was established in Baltimore.

June 2. The general assembly responded to a petition of inhabitants of the port of Baltimore County by having about twenty-five acres of land on the north and east side of Baltimore surveyed and laid out into lots and streets.

1751 A subscription was established to build a market house.

1752 The first agricultural fair was held on the grounds of John Edgar Howard's place on Greene Street.

1753 Andrew Steiger built a butcher shop.

April 30. A lottery drawing was held. Money was raised to build the public wharf.

November 17. The assembly passed an act empowering the commissioners of Baltimore to make an addition to the town of thirty-two acres of Cole's Harbor.

An act was passed prohibiting earth, sand, or dirt from being thrown into or put upon the beach or shore of the Patapsco River.

1754 Drs. John and Henry Stevenson arrived from Ireland. John

CHRONOLOGY

conducted trade with Ireland and other countries, while Henry practiced medicine. Both helped to develop Baltimore because of their faith in its growth.

February 4. Governor Horatio Sharpe, who had recently arrived in Maryland, visited Baltimore and was given a reception.

1755 — After General Braddock was defeated by the French and Indians, the Indians pushed within fifty miles of Baltimore.

Later that year, a large number of Acadians arrived in Maryland; some settled in Baltimore.

1756 — March 26. The general assembly passed an act raising large supplies for His Majesty's service to secure and protect frontiers of Maryland and arrange friendship with southern Indian tribes. Charles Carroll, Jr. was appointed one of the commissioners to deal with the Indians.

1757 — May. The Maryland assembly met in Baltimore because of a smallpox epidemic in Annapolis.

1758 — Jacob Mayers took a lot on the southeast corner of Gay and Baltimore streets on which to build an inn.

Mr. Grandchut erected a brewery on North Frederick Street.

1759 — John Smith from Ireland and William Buchanan from Carlisle bought a lot fronting on Gay and Water streets and built dwelling houses and two wharves.

1761 — James Sterrit from Lancaster, Pennsylvania, erected a brewery.

Meecher Heener arrived from Pennsylvania and built a warehouse below Hanover Street.

Mr. Lytle took a lot on the corner of Baltimore and Hanover streets, where he erected an inn.

1762 — April 24. The assembly passed an act empowering justices of Baltimore County Court to assess and levy £600 and 5 percent sheriff's fees for collection on taxable inhabitants of St. Paul's parish.

BALTIMORE

1763   John Brown from Jersey erected a pottery on Gay Street.

Samuel Purviance came from Donegal via Philadelphia and erected a distillery on the corner of Lombard and Commerce streets with a wharf.

A tobacco inspection house was built. The inspector paid 9,600 pounds of tobacco per year

A powder magazine was built on the corner of Calvert and Lexington streets.

Commissioners William Lyon, Nicholas R. Gay, John Moale, and Archibald leased a lot on the northwest corner of Baltimore and Gay streets at a rent of £8 per year to build a market house. A lottery was held to raise money for the building on July 16, 1763.

December 5. The Presbyterian meeting house was built. It was sold in 1765 to Charles Ridgely for £100 and accrued ground rent. It was used for a carpenter shop for many years.

1764   William Spear from Lancaster built a bakery.

Captain Charles Ridgely and Mr. Griffith bought water lots from Mr. Fell. Griffith built a wharf and a warehouse.

Benjamin Nelson, a shipwright, moved from Charlestown and established a shipyard on Philpot Street.

March. The Presbyterians purchased a lot at the northwest corner of Fayette and North streets. Their church building was completed in 1776.

September 17. The lower house of the assembly instructed William Murdock, Edward Tilghman, and Thomas Ringgold, Esqs. to join committees of several colonies to ask the king for relief from burden and restraints on trade, especially the taxes.

1766   A law was passed prescribing quarantine on passenger ships infected by diseases.

February 24. Inhabitants of Baltimore County organized the Maryland Sons of Liberty to maintain order. They decided

CHRONOLOGY

to meet at Annapolis on March 1 to force officials to transact business without stamped paper.

1768   George Patten built a wharf on the west end of the point.

June 22. An act was passed moving the county seat from Joppa to Baltimore.

1769   A committee aided by general subscription bought the first fire engine in Baltimore for £99, or $264.

Governor Robert Eden, successor to Governor Sharpe, arrived in Maryland with his wife, Caroline Calvert, and their children.

November 14. A meeting of merchants and others about nonimportation of European goods was held at Mr. Little's with John Smith as chairman.

1770   October 24. A Baltimore town meeting sent representatives to a meeting in Annapolis indicating that they would depart from nonimportation agreements as had merchants of Newport, Rhode Island, and Philadelphia.

1771   Jesse Hollingsworth built a wharf in the east end of town.

Jonathan Hanson was appointed inspector of flour.

1772   The first efforts were made in Baltimore to introduce the umbrella as protection from sun and rain. They were ridiculed. Physicians recommended them to ward off diseases, and then umbrellas were accepted.

The assembly authorized building the County Alms House.

November 28. Francis Asbury and Richard Wright, sent by John Wesley from England, preached in Baltimore.

1773   The assembly passed an act uniting Baltimore Town and the rival community of Fell's Point.

A large warehouse at the corner of Baltimore and Frederick streets was occasionally used as a theatre.

A line of packets and stage coaches was established to and from Philadelphia.

July. Messrs. Moale and Steiger were authorized to purchase eighteen acres of ground lying between Bridge and Front streets.

An advertisement appeared in the Maryland Gazette of the prospectus of the Maryland Journal and Baltimore Advertiser which was to be published in August.

August 20. The first issue of the Maryland Journal and Baltimore Advertiser appeared. It was later called the Baltimore Journal and Commercial Advertiser.

November. An act was passed appointing Charles Ridgely, William Lux, John Moale, William Smith, and Samuel Purviance of Baltimore Town and Andrew Buchanan and Harry Dorsey Gough as trustees for the poor of Baltimore County.

Jesse Hollingsworth, George Wells, Richard Moale, George Robinson, John Woodward, and others formed a society on Fell's Point that built the first Methodist meeting house in Baltimore.

1774

Isaac Griest, Benjamin Griffith, Jesse Hollingsworth, and thirteen others were appointed commissioners to direct spending of nearly $11,000 to build three great roads leading to Baltimore.

April 18. The foundation of the Methodist Church on Lovely Lane was laid.

May 31. The Baltimore Committee of Correspondence met in response to a plea of the people of Boston because of the closing of their port. Eight resolutions were passed in support of Boston.

August 23. A boat arrived from Baltimore at Marblehead under Captain Perkins to aid the poor people of Boston with 3,000 bushels of Indian corn, 20 barrels of rye, and 21 barrels of bread.

1775

May 2. The first number of Dunlap's Maryland Gazette or the Baltimore General Advertiser was issued weekly. Its name was changed in 1778 to the Maryland Gazette and Baltimore General Advertiser. It was discontinued January 5, 1779.

May 5. Hon. Peyton Randolph, Edmond Pendleton, Benjamin Harrison, Richard Henry Lee and George Washington lodged at Old Fountain Inn on their journey to Philadelphia as delegates to the Second Continental Congress.

July 13. A special town meeting in Baltimore was held; William Smith presided. A letter of James Christie, Jr., a merchant, was read. He asked for British troops to set things straight. The committee ordered guards around Christie's house forbidding any contact with him. He was declared a traitor at a meeting on August 9.

July 26. The Maryland Convention adopted the Articles of Association of Freemen of Maryland, which amounted to a practical declaration of independence. It provided for recruiting of troops.

October. Young Joshua Barney was the first individual to unfurl the Union flag in Maryland at Baltimore.

November. The scarcity of paper led William Goddard to establish a paper factory near town.

November 13. A committee was appointed to procure ammunition on the recommendation of the Continental Congress.

December. Congress authorized building the frigate <u>Virginia</u> in Mr. Well's shipyard. It was ready for sea in 1777. Baltimore was thus selected as a site for naval construction.

1776

March. The Whig Club was founded.

Captain Squires, commander of the British sloop of war <u>Otter</u>, gave a demonstration in Patapsco River, alarming citizens. Troops from Harford County marched to aid Baltimore.

July 6. The province of Maryland did not wait for the final Declaration of Independence from Congress. The Maryland Convention proclaimed independence.

July 29. The Declaration of Independence was read at the courthouse of Baltimore.

July 30. A meeting of the Baltimore Committee of Observation was held.

August 14. The state convention met at Annapolis to form a new constitution. For the first time Baltimore was represented separately from the county.

December 20. The Continental Congress held sessions in Baltimore at the house of Jacob Fite.

December 30. Congress authorized many men, including some from Baltimore, to sign bills of credit or money.

1777

An act of the legislature was passed requiring Baltimore Town and County to furnish 381 militia.

February. The Whig Club, a revolutionary society composed of radical members of the old committees, was formed in Baltimore.

May 5. News of an alliance between France and the United States reached Baltimore.

September 11. The Battle of Brandywine was fought with the Maryland Line present.

1778

March. Count Pulaski raised and fully organized an independent army corps in Baltimore.

1779

January. A committee of merchants was formed to provide suitable defense for private navigation of Chesapeake Bay.

February. Mr. Sterrit's large brewery and warehouse burned in a fire set by an incendiary.

November 6. Major-General Nathaniel Greene, new commander-in-chief of the Southern Army, passed through Baltimore.

1780

Fell's Prospect was first laid off by the commissioners and added to Baltimore on the east, as well as eighteen acres owned by Mr. Moale and Mr. Steiger.

August. Movements of Lord Cornwallis led to an alarm in Baltimore, which raised forces of 2800 to defend the city.

September 4. The French cutter Serpent under Amie de la Lanne arrived in Baltimore Harbor with despatches for General Washington from Count de Grasse, who arrived with the French fleet on September 26.

September 8. General Washington, Adjutant General Hand, and other officers arrived in Baltimore and stopped at the Fountain Inn.

1781 April 5. A meeting was held in the courthouse that set up a committee to provide defense for Baltimore because of the British concentration of forces near the mouth of the Chesapeake. Lafayette agreed to send men on the condition that he be advanced £10,000, to which the merchants speedily agreed.

August 7. A meeting was held at the courthouse. A committee was appointed to put new paper money ("red money") into circulation.

September 9. Major-General Count de Rochambeau, commander of the French troops in America under General Washington, stayed in Baltimore for a short period and proceeded south.

October 19. General Cornwallis surrendered to General Washington.

November 5. Marquis de Lafayette passed through Baltimore.

November 19. General and Mrs. Washington arrived in Baltimore and left the next day for Philadelphia.

1782 A public market was opened on Colonel Howard's estate.

Town officials began to pave streets and lay sidewalks in Baltimore, as well as to build additional wharves, and pass laws to guard streets. In addition, an auction tax, a tax on public exhibitions, and an assessed property tax was passed.

A stage coach line was established between Baltimore and Philadelphia by Gabriel Vanhorne, Nathaniel Twining, and others.

January 15. The first brick theatre in Baltimore was opened.

April 2. A notice appeared in <u>Maryland,</u> stating that inhabitants of Baltimore intended to petition the general assembly to incorporate the town.

August 3. Governor and Mrs. Thomas Sim Lee and others arrived from Annapolis. Count de Rochambeau reviewed the troops.

November. The general assembly approved additions to Baltimore including Gist's Inspection and Timber Neck, located south of earlier additions, as well as lands between Fell's Prospect and Harris's Creek. These were the last specified additions by an act of the assembly because the corporation was given power to admit other lands by consent of the owners.

1783 Samuel Smith, Samuel Purviance, Daniel Bowley, John Sterett, Thomas Russell, Richard Ridgely, Robert Henderson, Thomas Elliott, and William Patterson were appointed warders of the port of Baltimore, with Purviance as chairman. The group was authorized to survey and chart the basin, harbor, and Patapsco River, as well as to provide for clearing and measuring the channel, and to charge every vessel entering and leaving it.

A committee composed chiefly of Baltimoreans was formed and incorporated to make a canal to the Susquehanna River.

A regular stage coach line was established to Fredericktown and Annapolis.

John Jacob Astor arrived in Baltimore and shortly moved to New York.

February 19. The Journal published an extra, announcing, in advance of any paper in the country, the signing of preliminary articles of peace at Paris. The news was brought directly by the Baltimore Clipper.

April 11. Congress suspended hostilities. A celebration was held April 21.

May. Zachariah Allen was appointed first notary public in Baltimore.

May 16. The first number of the Maryland Gazette or the Baltimore Central Advertiser was published by John Hays as a weekly.

June 12. Major Barnet, an aide-de-camp to General Greene,

accompanied by Major Edwards, passed through Baltimore on his way to Philadelphia with dispatches to Congress announcing the evacuation of Charleston, South Carolina, by the British.

June 17. A convention of Freemasons was called into session at Talbot Courthouse. It passed a unanimous resolution to form a Grand Lodge for Maryland. The Freemasons met again on July 31 to elect grand officers.

June 22. The first convention of the diocese met and adopted a constitution that recognized the separation of church and state affairs.

July 27. Brigadier-General Mordecai Gist arrived from Annapolis with remnants of the Maryland Line, about 500 men.

September 30. Major-General Greene, accompanied by Major Hyrne, arrived in Baltimore from Charleston.

November 4. John Sterett's brewery burned down.

November 20-21. Officers of the Maryland Line met at Mr. Mann's Tavern in Annapolis. They instituted the Society of the Cincinnati, with Major-General Smallwood as president.

December. Thomas Peters arrived from Philadelphia and built a brewery.

December 18. General Washington addressed citizens on his way to Annapolis to resign his commission to Congress.

1784 The First Reformed Congregation purchased a lot on the corner of Baltimore and Front streets.

William Murphy, a bookseller, established a circulating library.

A new survey was ordered for Baltimore. Citizens began to discuss the need for a charter.

Messrs. Gart and Leypold built a sugar refinery on Peace Alley.

The general assembly incorporated a company to cut a canal from the basin at Charles Street to a cove in Ridgely's Addition.

July. Joshua Barney, the last officer retained by the army, resigned and returned to Baltimore.

September 1. Marquis de LaFayette was entertained in Baltimore.

November. The general assembly passed an act for establishment and regulation of a night watch and erection of street lamps in Baltimore.

1785 Captain Joseph White and others established regular packets to and from Norfolk, Virginia.

Colonel Howard and George Lux, Esq. gave a town lot on the west side of Baltimore for the internment of strangers.

March 23. Dr. John Stevenson, sixty-seven, died at his house in Market Street. He was considered one of the true founders of Baltimore because he helped it grow.

June 4. A general meeting of the Society of Friends (Quakers) was held in Baltimore. They returned in 1787 and 1789.

August. Construction was begun on the new Methodist Meeting House.

August 9. John O'Donnell, Esq. arrived from Canton on the ship Pallas with a full cargo of Chinese goods. It was the first direct importation from China to Baltimore.

September 1. The cornerstone for the First German Reform Church was laid.

1786 The Maryland Agricultural Society was organized and provided for an exhibit of products of the state.

The Association of Tradesmen and Manufacturers in Baltimore resolved to clothe themselves with home-manufactured goods.

March 3. A group of citizens met at Grant's Tavern to encourage and improve "agriculture and other branches of rural economy," electing Harry Dorsey Gough as president.

CHRONOLOGY

March 12. Andrew Buchanan, presiding justice of the county court, died.

August 17. The theatre built by Messrs. Hallam and Henry between Baltimore and the Point opened. The Old American Company performed The School for Scandal.

1787

The Maryland legislature passed laws to have several turnpikes laid out in Baltimore County: one toward Frederick, Maryland; a second with one branch toward Westminster, and the other branch toward Hanover, Pennsylvania; and a third to York, Pennsylvania.

A board was constituted to examine and license pilots.

Oliver Evans's newly invented steam carriage, elevator, and hopper-boy were patented by the assembly. The last two were introduced into mills around Baltimore.

The First Baltimore Light Infantry was recruited by Captain Mackeimer of the Continental Army.

March 17. Several fire companies, the Mechanical, Mercantile, Union, and Friendship, met at the house of Daniel Grant to establish regulations for fire-fighting, including responsibility of those not members of fire companies.

September 17. State delegates in Philadelphia completed the United States Constitution. The Maryland Convention ratified it on April 28, 1788. The Constitution went into effect in July 1788.

December 8. Cokesbury College (Methodist) opened in order to advance religion in America.

1788

The criminal court was organized for the county and town with five justices. Samuel Chase was appointed chief justice, with John Moale, William Russell, Otto H. Williams, and Lyde Goodwin as associate justices.

Fall. The Chesapeake of Baltimore was the first American vessel allowed to hoist the colors of the United States in the River Ganges and to trade in India.

1789

The earliest general meeting of the Roman Catholic Clergy of the United States in Baltimore decided to request the

Pope to establish an Episcopal See in Baltimore. Rev. Dr. Carroll was recommended as a suitable person for the office of chief pastor. Carroll went to Europe to receive consecration.

March 3. A petition from shipwrights and other inhabitants of Baltimore, men who had built Joshua Barney's Federalist, requested that a mercantilist system like England's be adopted.

April 17. President-elect George Washington arrived in Baltimore on his way to New York. A reception was held at the Fountain Inn.

May 14. The Baltimore American and Daily Advertiser began publication.

November 6. A group of physicians in Baltimore formed the Medical Society of Baltimore with Dr. Edward Johnson, president.

1790

The population of Baltimore was 13,503.

Medical lectures were delivered during the course of the year.

Messrs. Caton, Vanbibber, A. McKim Townsend, and others formed an association to manufacture cotton, as well as jeans and velvet.

May 7. The first session of the Circuit Court of the United States for the district was held in Baltimore by John Blair, justice of the Supreme Court, and William Pace, district judge.

August. The consecration of the new Roman Catholic bishop, Dr. Carroll, was performed in the chapel of Ludworth Castle, England by Rev. Charles Walmsley, bishop of Rama.

September. Papering walls of houses was first introduced. People had previously used whitewash.

November. The general assembly authorized a group to take subscriptions for the Bank of Maryland. At $100 per share, $200,000 was authorized. William Patterson was named president and Ebenezer Mackie, cashier. The entire capital of $300,000 was soon paid in.

CHRONOLOGY 17

1791 Bishop Carroll held a diocesan synod in Baltimore where several decrees of discipline were enacted.

Robert Gilmor, John O'Donnell, Stephen Wilson, Charles Chequier, John Holmes, and others built a powder house on Gwinn's Falls.

Benjamin Nicholson was appointed chief judge of Baltimore, with General Williams and James Carroll as judges.

William Buchanan, Campbell Smith, and George Chase took commissions for defense of the frontiers.

July 4. A lecture on the moral and political evil of slavery was delivered at a public meeting of the Maryland Society for promoting Abolition of Slavery and Relief of Free Negroes and Others Unlawfully Held in Bondage.

October 24. The first number of the Baltimore Daily Repository was issued as the first daily paper in Baltimore by David Graham.

December 27. The general assembly authorized Elisha Tyson, William and Charles Jessop, John Ellicott, George Legett, Robert Long, Jacob Hart, and John Striker to lay out a road from mill seats on Jones Falls to Baltimore.

December 30. Alexander Rigson, John Stump, John Carlile, John Wetson, Samuel Raine, John Treadway, and James Johnson were appointed commissioners to lay out Philadelphia, Belair, and Harford roads as public roads.

1792 Several military companies were raised.

An assembly was incorporated of clergymen and ministers of different sects or churches to give alms to the poor of every religious society.

February. The Baltimore branch of the Bank of the United States was opened.

July 27. A number of citizens met to indicate disapproval of Jay's treaty with Great Britain. A committee was appointed to indicate their views to President Washington.

December 23. The assembly passed an act permitting the

Maryland Insurance Company to supply Baltimore with water by pipes from the reservoir, to be called the Baltimore Water Company.

1793   December 28. The general assembly passed an act appointing commissioners to lay off ten acres of land in or near Baltimore as a market for cattle, horses, sheep, and hogs.

1794   The fort at Whetstone Point was repaired in response to the embargo. Brickwork was added. Ground was ceded to the United States government and was called Fort McHenry in honor of Col. James McHenry of Maryland, then secretary of war.

January 1. The Maryland Abolition Society sent delegates to the first Convention of Abolition Societies at Philadelphia.

May. The first session of the Grand Masonic Lodge met in Baltimore.

Summer. Yellow Fever broke out. During August and September 344 people died.

September 25. Mr. Wignell and his partner Mr. Reinagle opened the New Theatre in Baltimore.

November. Five hundred men from Baltimore under Major-General Smith were sent to quell the Whiskey Insurrection in Pennsylvania.

1795   January 1. Phillip Edwards, editor, began daily publication of the Baltimore Daily Advertiser.

March 2. John W. Allen issued the first number of the Fell's Point Telegraph, a triweekly.

March 23. Clayland, Dobbin and Company issued the first number of the Baltimore Telegraph. It was later continued by Thomas Dobbin under the name of the Telegraph and Daily Advertiser.

December 4. The Methodist Cokesbury College was destroyed by fire. The large assembly hall or ballroom on the lot where the late Light Street Church stood was purchased.

CHRONOLOGY

December 24. The assembly passed an act incorporating the Bank of Baltimore. The Maryland Fire Insurance Company was also incorporated.

December 26. The general assembly incorporated the Baltimore Equitable Society to insure houses from losses by fire.

1796

The <u>Eagle</u> <u>of</u> <u>Freedom</u> was published by Pechin and Wilmer.

Messrs. Thompson and Walker issued the first directory published in Baltimore containing names, occupation, and residence of inhabitants of Balitmore and Fell's Point.

The Charitable Marine Society was formed and incorporated in the name of Thomas Elliott, David Porter, Thomas Cole, Daniel Howland, and others, including masters of ships, or their friends.

January 1. The <u>Federal</u> <u>Intelligencer</u> changed its name to the <u>Federal</u> <u>Gazette</u> <u>and</u> <u>Baltimore</u> <u>Daily</u> <u>Advertiser</u>.

January 20. President Washington appointed Samuel Chase as justice of the United States Supreme Court.

July 4. The first meeting of the Society of the Cincinnati was held at the Indian Queen Hotel.

October 22. The Baltimore Library Company opened a library for the use of members at the house of Mr. Williams.

December 31. The assembly passed an act incorporating the City of **Baltimore** as an experiment for one year only. It also passed an act to lay out and establish a turnpike road from Washington to Baltimore.

BALTIMORE CITY

1797

The Second Baptist Church was founded.

A local ordinance was passed requiring inspection of flour.

The mayor and the city council appointed Richard H. Moale to maintain Baltimore records and William Gipson to keep all the funds of the city.

Captain David Porter, Sr. established the Signal House, a hall for dancing.

A subscription raised money to build the Assembly Room, a hall for dancing.

January 5. Baltimore was divided into eight wards.

January 20. The general assembly passed acts incorporating the German Evangelical Church, the Presbyterian Church, and the Library Company of Baltimore, which later merged with the Maryland Historical Society. The legislature also passed an act to lay out and establish a turnpike from Baltimore through Fredericktown to Elizabethtown and Williamsport, and incorporated Reistertown Turnpike Company.

February 21. Electors met and elected James Calhoun as mayor, and eight members to the Second Branch of the City Council.

May 10. Thorowgood Smith was elected mayor to fill the unexpired term of James Calhoun.

September 19. The United States frigate <u>Constellation</u> was launched at the navy yard of David Stodder. Captain Thomas Truxton commanded her.

1798

The prospect of war led to filling up old militia companies and forming new ones.

September 8. The first antislavery society in the state of Maryland was founded. Philip Rogers was elected president.

1799

The general assembly passed an act agreeing to the construction of a canal connecting the Chesapeake and Delaware bays, if Pennsylvania would declare the Susquehanna River a public highway and authorize the removal of obstructions to navigation.

June 3. The United States sloop-of-war <u>Maryland</u> was launched from Price's ship yard at Fell's Point.

June 4. The Baltimore races began at a new course on Whetstone Point.

June 20. The United States sloop-of-war <u>Chesapeake</u> was launched from De Rochbroom's ship yard at Fell's Point.

July 24. A committee was appointed to raise funds by subscription to finish fortifications at Fort McHenry.

August 18. Honeycomb was published by Alexander Martin, editor of American. It was a literary paper of eight pages.

1800   The population of Baltimore was 26,514.

Marcus McCausland erected a brewery on Holliday Street.

A new powder magazine was built on the south side of the river.

June 15. President John Adams passed through Baltimore from Washington.

December 19. The legislature passed an act authorizing the mayor and the city council of Baltimore to introduce water into the city.

1801   William Taylor and his physician, Dr. M. Littlejohn, spread information about innoculation to prevent smallpox. Dr. James Smith introduced innoculation generally and convinced the legislature to sanction its distribution.

Emanuel Kent, Elisha Tyson, William Maccreery, Richardson Stewart, and others formed a society to furnish free medicinal relief to the poor.

January 7. The first regular meeting of the Female Humane Association for the relief of indigent women was held at the residence of Bishop Carroll.

December 1. The first number of the Republican or Anti-Democrat, a triweekly, was published by Messrs. Prentiss and Cole.

1802   September 25. The first regular issue of the American Patriot was published by S. McCrea. The company moved to Fell's Point, where its name was changed to the American Patriot and Fell's Point Advertiser.

1803   Reverend Bishop Carroll and Mr. James Priestley obtained a charter for Baltimore College, to be built by the aid of a lottery.

The Union Bank of Maryland was organized and chartered. William Winchester was president and Ralph Higginbotham, cashier.

December 24. Jerome Bonaparte, youngest brother of Napoleon, was married to Miss Elizabeth Patterson, eldest daughter of William Patterson, Esq.

1804

The Union Bank and the Farmers and Merchants Bank were chartered with a capital of $3,000,000 and $1,000,000, respectively.

The commissioners purchased ground and erected buildings on Madison Street for the confinement of prisoners. In 1809 a criminal code was adopted, leaving only the crimes of murder, arson, rape and treason liable to the death penalty.

January 1. Alexander Martin began publication of Rush-Light, a satirical, political, and literary weekly.

April 30. The Baltimore Water Company was formed with capital of $250,000. Stock sold for over 900 percent above par.

August. The Porcupine was established.

November 3. The first number of Companion and Weekly Miscellany was issued by Edward Essy, Esq.

November 5. Thorowgood Smith was reelected mayor.

1805

An act of the assembly appointed commissioners to build a new courthouse. Thomas McElderry, Henry Payson, William Jessop, Alexander McKim, Jr., Thomas Rutter, Robert Stewart, and William C. Goldsmith were appointed.

January. St. Mary's College of Baltimore was raised to the rank of university by the Maryland Legislature.

March 25. The first number of the Baltimore Evening Post and Mercantile Daily Advertiser was issued by J. Cook and Company.

1806

The Mercantile Bank was incorporated.

Messrs. Sower and Hewes established a type foundry.

CHRONOLOGY 23

July 7. A ceremony of blessing and laying of the cornerstone of the Roman Catholic cathedral was held.

1807   Robert Gilmor became president of a company organized to import goods from Calcutta and China.

Frame buildings were prohibited from being erected in the central and improved part of the city.

Drs. Davidge, Shaw, and Cocke were granted permission to establish a medical college and to raise funds by lottery to erect buildings.

December 23. Congress established a general embargo that lasted until March 16, 1809.

1808   The city hospital was leased by the mayor and council to Drs. McKenzie and Smyth and survivors for fifteen years. The term was extended to twenty-five years in 1814.

The Tammany Political Club was organized.

A society was formed to manufacture cotton goods. It built a factory on the Patapsco River.

January. The first number of the <u>North American and Mercantile Daily Advertiser</u> was issued by Jacob Wagner.

February 8. Property qualifications of members of the First Branch of the City Council were reduced to $300, and for mayor and second branch to $500.

October 4. Several pipes of gin from Holland were burned because they had been subjected to duties in England.

November. Edward Johnson was elected mayor.

1809   John Comegys, James Buchanan, David Winchester, and others asked the legislature for permission to raise $100,000 to erect a monument in memory of George Washington on the grounds of the old courthouse.

The Carpenters' Humane Society was granted a charter.

1810   March. The following banks were chartered because the Charter of the Bank of the United States was expiring and would probably not be renewed: the Commercial and Farmers Bank, the Farmers and Merchants Bank, the Franklin Bank, and the National Maritime Bank.

1811

The Humane Impartial Society received a charter.

The City Bank, with a capital of $39,405 in private stock, raised without the sanction of the state, was opened.

Alexander Brown and Sons, a private bank, was opened.

The city council gave authority to the mayor and city commissioners to borrow $25,000 toward construction of stone bridges at Pratt and Gay streets.

September 7. The first issue of Niles' Register was published by Hezekiah Niles. It was read throughout the world. On September 3, 1836, Hezekiah gave up the business to his eldest son, William Ogden Niles, who continued to publish the Register in an enlarged form. The office was moved to Washington, D.C., on September 2, 1837, where the paper was published under the name of Niles National Register. The office moved back to Baltimore May 4, 1839, where it continued to be published until February 28, 1848, when it ceased to exist.

1812

A battalion of infantry marched to Fort McHenry for training twice a week under Major-General Smith.

The Bible Society was formed and chartered with James McHenry as president.

Thomas Warner was appointed assayer of **manufactured** plate by the city government.

Rembrandt Peale fixed his permanent residence in Baltimore. He began building a museum and gallery of fine arts.

May 21. A meeting of Democratic delegates from wards and precincts criticized both the British and French for their actions.

June 18. A formal declaration of war against Great Britain was **announced.** The act had been passed June 8. This led to much volunteering for the army in Baltimore.

July 26. The first English vessel, Fanny, arrived at Baltimore as a prize to the privateer Dolphin. The cargo was valued at $18,000.

December 15. The legislature passed an act annulling the marriage of Jerome and Elizabeth Bonaparte.

December 31. The City Bank of Baltimore was incorporated with an authorized capital of $1,500,000.

1813   Rembrandt Peal set up a small gas plant to illuminate his gallery. He used this as a selling point in 1816 to organize a company to sell gas in Baltimore.

The British entered Chesapeake Bay early in the year. The Baltimore Corporation appointed a committee of supply to spend $20,000 for defense. The committee recommended raising a loan of $50,000 for this purpose.

Mr. Flanigan built the first steamboat, Chesapeake, at the end of McElderry's Wharf for William McDonald and Company. It was put on the line from Baltimore to Philadelphia.

Charles Gwinn introduced steam power for a flour mill in his warehouse at the end of Commerce Street Wharf. Mr. Job introduced steam power in a saw mill on Chase's Wharf.

May 10. The New Theatre, later called the Holliday Street Theatre, was opened.

1814   January 31. Commodore Stephen Perry stopped in Baltimore for three days.

September 12. A battle occurred at Fell's Point.

September 13. The battle was fought for Fort McHenry. Francis Scott Key went out into the harbor on the ship Minden under a flag of truce. Key was placed on board the Surprise then back on the Minden, anchored in sight of the Fort. He wrote the words for "The Star Spangled Banner," which he finally wrote out when he returned to Baltimore. His Uncle Judge Nicholson had it printed at the Baltimore American offices. It was first sung in Baltimore by Charles Durang, who set it to music, in the presence of the defenders of the city at a restaurant next to the Holliday Theatre. It was published in the Baltimore American, September 21.

1815   William Patterson, Robert G. Harper, Dennis A. Smith, John Oliver, Thomas Tennant, Robert Smith, Henry Payson, Isaac McKim, Henry Thompson, and others purchased grounds on Front Street and began building the Exchange. The United States government purchased part of the grounds for a customs house.

February 15. Baltimore celebrated the news of peace with Britain along with the news of the repulse of the British at New Orleans.

March. The first number of the Mechanics' Gazette and Merchants' Daily Advertiser was issued by Thomas Wilson and Company.

March 1. The Committee of Vigilance and Safety of the City of Baltimore announced plans to erect a monument in memory of those who fell in battle. The cornerstone was to be laid September 12.

June. Rev. John Francis Moranville, pastor of St. Patrick's Church, founded a school of education for poor females, the St. Patrick's Benevolent Society.

July 4. The cornerstone of Washington Monument was laid in Howard's Park.

December 3. The Right Reverend John Carroll, D.D. died. He had been the first Roman Catholic bishop in the United States.

1816   The legislature passed an act to annex the so-called Precincts to Baltimore with consent of 9/10 of both.

Rev. Dr. James Kemp became bishop of the diocese and the first Episcopal bishop residing in Baltimore.

Jonathan Meredith, Thomas Kell, and D. Hoffman appointed insolvent commissioners to examine applicants and grant provisional relief.

Subscriptions to the new Bank of the United States was opened with a capital of $28 million. $4,014,000 was subscribed in Baltimore.

January 29. Maryland Hospital was incorporated.

February 1. Saint Andrew's Society of Baltimore was incorporated. The Medical Society of Maryland was also incorporated.

May 25. The first number of the People's Friend was issued.

June 19. The mayor and city council passed an ordinance granting permission to the Gas Light Company of Baltimore to more effectively light the streets of Baltimore. A charter was obtained February 5, 1817.

November. George Stiles was elected mayor. He resigned February 9, 1819.

1817 Sunday schools were established by various sects.

A society was formed to aid the Colonization Society, established at Washington, to procure voluntary transportation of free blacks to the coast of Africa.

February 10. A meeting was held at the house of Henry Payson to form a religious society and build a new church for Unitarians.

February 11. The Hibernian Society of Baltimore was incorporated.

February 16. The second dispensary was incorporated by the legislature.

April 15. The New York legislature authorized construction of the Erie Canal, which was completed in 1825. It was to take commerce away from Baltimore and other cities.

June 18. Rev. Leonard Neale, second bishop of Baltimore, died. He was succeeded by Rev. Ambrose Marechal.

July 28. The First Mechanical Volunteers built a monument to the memory of Aquilla Randall, one of its members who fell on the battlefield at North Point.

1818 March 16. The Savings Bank was incorporated with Captain Daniel Howland, president.

1819 The American Farmer was the first agricultural journal published in the United States and perhaps in the world.

February 9. Mayor George Stiles resigned.

February 16. Edward Johnson was elected mayor to fill Stiles's unexpired term.

February 27. General Andrew Jackson arrived in Baltimore.

April. The <u>Commercial</u> <u>Chronicle</u> was first published.

April 13. John Welch, John Duncan, John Cheathan, and Richard Rushworth met at Thomas Wildey's dwelling and arranged for formation of the Lodge of Odd Fellows. They met at the tavern on Fell's Point on April 26 and organized the first Odd Fellows' Lodge, calling it Washington Lodge Number 1.

October 23. The <u>Red</u> <u>Book</u> was published anonymously by John P. Kennedy, Peter Cruse and Josiah Pennington.

October 25. An encampment that had been set up near the city as a result of fear of the yellow fever epidemic which raged during the summer was finally broken up.

1820   The population of Baltimore was 62,738

James Ball of Baltimore bequeathed to the president and directors of the Bank of Maryland $5,000 in trust to establish a free school in the city on the plan of the Boston schools.

John Montgomery was elected mayor.

June. The Exchange Building was opened for business. The great hall was filled with merchants of the city who agreed to meet at a certain hour of the day to carry on business.

September 7. The presidents of several banks of Baltimore met and resolved on September 16 not to issue or reissue any notes less than $5 and not to receive in payment, or on deposit, any notes but their own.

1821   The Merchants' Bank was incorporated with Robert Gilmor as president.

May 31. The Roman Catholic cathedral which was begun in 1806 was consecrated.

1822	Edward Johnson was elected mayor.

Mr. T. Poppleton prepared a map of the whole city and harbor.

The Apprentice's Library was formed to loan useful books to youths of the city. Col. James Mosher was named president.

February 25. William Pinckney died. He had been a United States attorney-general, as well as minister to Russia and envoy to Naples.

September 12. A statue was placed on Battle Monument.

December 2. The New Alms House at Calverton, two miles west of the city, was opened. |
| 1823 | John Olliver left a bequest of $20,000 to the Hibernian Society, of which he was president, to establish a free school in Baltimore for the education of children of both sexes, without distinction as to religious tenets.

December 21. A town meeting was held in the rotunda of the Exchange, at which citizens decided to have the canal go from Baltimore to the Susquehanna, rather than the Ohio River. The assembly passed an act accordingly. Another act was passed incorporating a company to build a canal from the tidewater of the Potomac to the Ohio River. |
| 1824 | John Montgomery was elected mayor

August 10. The cornerstone of the Baltimore Athenaeum was laid.

October 7. Marquis de LaFayette arrived in Baltimore on board the ship United States, along with Secretary of State John Quincy Adams, and left for Washington, October 11. |
| 1825 | The following societies were incorporated: the Academy of Sciences, Robert Gilmor, president; the Maryland Institute of Arts, W. Stewart, president; the Pennsylvania, Delaware and Maryland Steam Navigation Company; the Lafayette Beneficial Company; the Fireman's Insurance Company; Patapsco Fire Engine Company; Aetna Company for manufacturing iron; and the Seaman's Union. |

A line of packets was established between Baltimore, Charleston, Savannah, and New Orleans.

D. Barnum, W. Shipley, and J. Philips, Jr. began to build Barnum's City Hotel.

December 14. A meeting of delegates of counties of Maryland was held to deliberate on measures for internal improvement of the state. They proposed to build a canal from Baltimore, to intersect and unite with the Chesapeake and Ohio Canal, then to Pittsburgh and on to Lake Erie.

1826   Jacob Small was elected mayor.

February. The legislature authorized the City of Baltimore to establish a system of public schools. No schools were actually in operation until 1829.

February 16. The Maryland Academy of Science and Literature was incorporated; it eventually moved to the Athanaeum.

Fall. Col. John Eager Howard held a meeting and dinner at his home, Belvidere. Evan Thomas, brother of Philip E. Thomas, president of the Merchants' Bank, was the guest of honor. He told of the Darlington and Stockton Steam Railroad in England. He was convinced that a railroad was the answer to the Erie Canal.

November 7. The first exhibition of the Maryland Institute was held at a hall in South Charles Street.

1827   January 9. The city council unanimously passed a bill adopting a law of the legislature relative to the establishment of public schools.

February 28. Baltimore procured a charter for the Baltimore and Ohio Railroad. It was confirmed by Virginia on March 8, and by Pennsylvania on February 28, 1828.

March 20. Subscription books were opened for the purchase of stock of the Baltimore and Ohio Railroad. The Corporation of Baltimore took 5,000 shares. The city alone subscribed $4,178,000.

April 24. The first railroad company in the United States

was organized. The cornerstone for its headquarters was laid July 4, 1828.

November 20. Surveys were begun for the Baltimore and Ohio Railroad by the Corps of Engineers.

December 3. The first number of the Marylander was issued by friends of President John Quincy Adams. It was discontinued after the election of 1828 when Adams lost.

1828

Two steamboat lines were begun: one to Washington and Alexandria, Virginia, and the other for Baltimore, Norfolk, Petersburg, and Richmond, Virginia.

January 29. Archbishop Ambrose Marechal died.

February 13. The Maryland legislature incorporated the Baltimore and Susquehanna Railroad from Baltimore to the Pennsylvania state line in the direction of York. Work was begun on August 8, 1829.

March. Subscriptions for the Baltimore and Susquehanna Railroad were opened with more than the required number of shares, although Pennsylvania would not sanction the road going through the state because of competition with its canal.

May 26. General Swift and George Winchester left Baltimore to make reconnaissance of the country between Baltimore and the Susquehanna, preparatory to beginning the survey.

June. Evan Poultney opened a banking house in Baltimore.

July 4. The promoters of the Chesapeake and Ohio Canal arranged a cornerstone laying. They persuaded President John Quincy Adams to wield the trowel. The Baltimore and Ohio Railroad called on Charles Carroll of Carrollton, surviving signer of the Declaration of Independence, to lay its cornerstone.

November 12. The Itinerant or Methodist Visitor was first published by Melville B. Cox, editor.

1829

The following publications were first issued: Mutual Rights and Christian Intelligencer, Itinerant Weekly, and Saturday Evening Post.

Charters were granted for a congregation of Jews, the Rapoahinck Steam Packet Company, the Sugar Refining Company, as well as the Howard Company.

June 5. The Sisters of Providence, a religious society of black women, established a school for black girls in Baltimore.

September. John S. Skinner began publication of the <u>American Turf Register and Sporting Magazine</u>.

September 10. The New Theatre and Circus was opened with 3,000 attending.

September 24. Four new schools were opened, one each for males and females in eastern and western parts of the city.

October 6. A meeting was held at the Athenaeum to form a temperance society with the Honorable Judge Brice as chairman.

October 29. The Roman Catholic Council held a session in Baltimore.

November 25. The managers raised the last piece of statue to the summit of the Washington Monument.

December 4. Charles Carroll of Carrollton laid the last stone of the viaduct at Gwynn's Falls. The president and directors resolved to name it Carrollton Viaduct.

1830   The Quaker Meeting House was built in Baltimore.

January 1. A party of ladies and gentlemen, including Postmaster General Wirt, rode in a carriage drawn by a single horse from the city terminus to the Carrollton Viaduct at a speed of fifteen miles an hour.

January 7. The Railroad was opened to the general public. It was the first time in the United States that a railroad operated as a common carrier.

August 28. "Tom Thumb," Peter Cooper's steam engine, was given a test run on the Baltimore and Ohio Railroad on a trip to Ellicott's Mills.

September. The first fatal accident on the Baltimore and Ohio Railroad occurred because of the bad conduct of a horse. The driver was killed.

November. William Stewart was elected mayor.

1831

The Methodist Protestant was first published by W.C. Dulany.

April 26. The Odd Fellows of Baltimore celebrated their anniversary in the city with the dedication of a new hall in Gay Street..

July 4. The Baltimore and Susquehanna Railroad was opened for public travel.

September 26. An anti-Masonic convention met in Baltimore with 126 delegates present. It was formed as a means of destroying Masonry. William Wirt was nominated for president on September 28, and Amos Ellmakeer of Pennsylvania for vice president.

November. Mrs. Mary Barney issued the first number of her political and literary monthly called the National Magazine or Lady's Companion.

December 12. The National Republican **Convention** met in Baltimore at the Athenaeum with 140 present. Henry Clay was unanimously nominated for president on December 13, and John Sergent of Pennsylvania was nominated for vice president on December 14.

1832

February. Messrs. Cloud and Wilman published the first number of the Saturday Visitor.

March 6. The Western National Bank was chartered.

March 15. The Chesapeake Bank of Baltimore was organized. Its books were opened for subscription on May 8.

May 1. The cornerstone of St. James' Roman Catholic Church was laid.

May 21. The Jackson General Convention met at the Athenaeum to nominate Andrew Jackson for president, and on May 22, Martin Van Buren of New York for vice president.

Summer. An outbreak of cholera occurred, continuing through September with many deaths.

November. Jesse Hunt was elected mayor.

November 13. The Horticultural Society was formed at the office of the <u>American Farmer</u>. B.I. Cohen was elected chairman.

November 14. Charles Carroll of Carrollton died.

December 27. The citizens of Baltimore met at the Exchange to discuss the proceedings of the nullification convention in South Carolina. They indicated disapproval of nullification.

1833   March 6. The Second National Bank was incorporated as the Fell's Point Savings Institution. It was converted into the Eastern Bank of Baltimore, and on March 8, 1864 it was chartered by an act of the assembly as the National Bank.

May 4. A new line of steamers began operations between Baltimore and Philadelphia.

June. President Jackson visited Baltimore. He had an interview with the celebrated Indian chief Black Hawk and other Indians.

June 12. The Horticultural Society of Maryland held its first exhibition.

1834   Messrs. J.F. Weishampel, Sr. and J.J. Beach published <u>The Experiment</u>.

March 24. The directors of the Bank of Maryland declared the bank's inability to continue its business. Officers of other banks met at the Union Bank, and were informed by the president of the Union Bank, Mr. Ellicott, that the Bank of Maryland was ready to deliver all property of the bank to him in trust. The meeting decided unanimously that Mr. Ellicott should accept.

April 30. The United States Insurance Company suspended payment.

May 6. The Maryland Savings Institutuion suspended operations, causing a severe run upon the Savings Bank of Baltimore.

May 7. Pursuant to a call from the Jackson Republican Convention of Baltimore, a meeting of friends of the national administration was called. It was held May 15.

October 19. Archbishop James Whitfeld died.

November 11. A new locomotive engine, built by Charles Reeder of Baltimore for the Baltimore and Ohio Railroad, exploded on a trial trip. This was the first locomotive explosion.

1835 Messrs. Clark and Kellogg established a new line of packets to run between Baltimore and New Orleans.

February 13. The courthouse was nearly destroyed by fire.

March 11. The Merchants' National Bank was incorporated.

April 15. The Pennsylvania Legislature created the York and Wrightsville Railroad Company, to connect with the Pennsylvania State works and become a link from either Philadelphia or Pittsburgh to Baltimore.

May 20. The Great Council of Maryland of the Tribe of Red Men was organized in Baltimore by George A. Peters, William F. Jones, Charles Skillman, Joseph Bronson, and Edmund Lucas.

The National Democratic Convention met in Baltimore, nominating Martin Van Buren as candidate for president, and Col. Richard M. Johnson for vice president.

June 15. The cornerstone was laid for the Episcopal Church of Ascension.

June 27. A violent rainstorm caused much damage. Thomas Marshall, son of the chief justice of the United States Supreme Court, John Marshall, was hurt in the crash of a building and died several days later.

August 7. Mayor Jesse Hunt called for a meeting to preserve peace because of the pamphlet war by Evan Poultney, former president of the Bank of Maryland and others, which had led to violence on August 6.

August 8. A riot broke out again, which led to anarchy. An

assembly of citizens chose eighty-three-year-old General Samuel Smith as chairman. He was able to restore order.

August 12. Mayor Hunt resigned. General Smith was elected mayor on September 7.

August 25. The Baltimore and Washington Railroad was formally opened.

1836

Messrs. Cloud and Powder first published the Daily Intelligencer.

The Family Magazine was first published.

The Maryland Academy of Science and Literature was revived with Patrick Macaulay as president.

An act of the legislature was passed increasing the Baltimore delegation from two to four members.

Horace Abbot moved to Baltimore and bought the Canton Iron Works from Peter Cooper. Abbott forged the first large steamship shaft in the United States for the Russian frigate Kamtschatka.

February 29. The firm of Swain, Abell and Simmons was founded to publish the Times in Philadelphia. On March 25, 1836, the firm established the Sun in Baltimore.

March 10. The first one-cent paper appeared in Baltimore, the Baltimore Daily Transcript. It was founded by S.P. Kenney and A.G. Teny.

March 15. **Baltimore's mayor and city council resolved** to subscribe to $3 million of capital stock of the Baltimore and Ohio Railroad.

April 2. The Citizens' National Bank was founded.

April 4. The National Bankers and Planters' Bank of Baltimore was incorporated.

October 8. The first number of the Monument, a weekly journal, was issued.

1837

May 12. The banks of Baltimore, following those of Philadelphia and New York, suspended specie payments.

May 17. The first copy of the Sun appeared.

June 20. The Chesapeake and Ohio Canal began to issue change of notes.

June 29. The City Council of Baltimore passed an ordinance authorizing issue of certificates for small sums to the amount of $350,000.

1838

The German paper, Geschäftige Martha, was published.

February 3. The Baltimore Theatre and Circus was destroyed by fire.

February 5. The Articles of Union were agreed upon by the Wilmington and Susquehanna Railroad Company, the Baltimore and Port Deposit Railroad Company, and the Philadelphia, Wilmington and Baltimore Railroad Company, creating one corporation: the Philadelphia, Wilmington, and Baltimore Railroad Company.

March 3. The Baltimore Price Current first appeared, published by William G. Lyford.

August. The railroad from Baltimore to York was opened.

November. **The Convent of the Visitation with an academy,** established by eleven sisters, was transferred from Georgetown to Baltimore.

Sheppard C. Leakin was elected mayor.

1839

The following were first published: the Penny Magazine, the Journal of the American Silk Society, the Baltimore Literary Monument, and the Baltimore Post.

July 13. **Greenmount** Cemetary was dedicated.

September 7. The first number of the Baltimore Clipper was issued by John H. Hewitt and Company.

October 10. Officers of Baltimore banks met following news of suspension of specie payment by Philadelphia banks, to adopt a plan to ward off heavy drafts from other cities.

November 14. The **Mercantile** Library Association was established with J. Morrison Harris as president.

BALTIMORE

December 16. The Manual Labor School was founded at the First Baptist Church, with Dr. Dunbar, chairman.

1840

Charles F. and R.M. Cloud first issued the Argus. They purchased the Republican in 1841 and consolidated it as the Republican and Argus.

The first issue of a German paper, the Wahrheits Verbreiter, was published.

May 5. The National Democratic Convention met at the Assembly Rooms, nominating Martin Van Buren for president, leaving vice presidential candidate selection to the states.

May 13. The president and directors of the Susquehanna Railroad and citizens celebrated completion of the road to Wrightsville, Pennsylvania.

May 14. The Whig Convention opened, nominating William Henry Harrison for president.

June 27. The Baltimore Clipper published the first issue of a weekly called the Ocean.

August. The first number of the Whig Penny sheet, the Daily Evening Gazette, was issued by William Ogden Niles, Esq.

August 1. The Spirit of Democracy was first published by R. M. Cloud.

November 2. Samuel Borady was elected mayor.

1841

January. The United States Catholic Monthly Magazine and Monthly Review was first issued by John Murphy, publisher, and Rev. Charles J. White, editor.

February 2. Frederick Rains founded the German Correspondent.

April. The Independent Press, a triweekly, was first published.

August. The Clayite, an evening paper, was founded.

The Baltimore Counterfeit Detector was first issued by H. Wigman.

November. The first numbers of the following were issued: the Christian Family Magazine, the Baltimore Privateer, and the Baltimore Phoenix and Budget.

1842   April 15. The Baltimore Steam Packet Company's Medora was making its first run when the boiler exploded, killing many people

July. The Baltimore Whig was founded.

October 23. G.W. Webb, William J. Heuisler, and others met at St. Peter's School House to form the Young Catholic Friend's Society, with Reverend McColgan as chairman.

November. Solomon Hillen, Jr. was elected mayor.

November 10. A train of cars containing the president and directors of the Baltimore and Ohio Railroad left Baltimore to travel the length of the road to Cumberland.

1843   September 18. The new Odd Fellows' Hall was dedicated.

November. Samuel Shoemaker of Baltimore entered into partnership with Alvin Adams of Boston, W.B. Dinsmore of New York, and Edward S. Sanford of Philadelphia, to open the Adams and Company Express Line between the cities mentioned.

November 6. Ceremonies were held attending the embarkation of eighty male and female black emigrants sent out by the Maryland Colonization Society to the colony of Cape Palmas on board the Latrobe.

1844   The Democratic Whig, a German paper, was first published by William Raine.

The American Journal of Insanity was founded by Johns Hopkins Press.

January 27. A meeting was held in the Colonization Society rooms to form the Historical Society with John J. Donaldson as chairman.

February 1. The first regular meeting of the Historical Society of Maryland elected General J. Spear Smith president.

April 6. The first number of the Democratic Sentinel was published.

May. Omnibuses began running from one end of Baltimore to the other, offering cheap transportation.

May 1. The Whig National Nominating Convention assembled in the Universalist Church, nominating Henry Clay for president, and Theodore Freylinghuysen of New Jersey for vice president.

May 20. The Magnetic Telegraph from Washington to the railroad depot on Pratt Street was completed.

May 27. The Tyler National Convention met at the Odd Fellows' Hall, nominating James K. Polk for president and George M. Dallas for vice president on May 30, in place of Silas M. Wright, who was nominated for vice president, but refused to accept.

Dr. Colton gave the first demonstration of laughing gas in the Assembly Rooms.

November. Jacob G. Davies was elected mayor.

November 11. The Baltimore Clipper's name was changed to the American Republican.

December 3. Jackson Square was donated to the city.

1845   P.T. Barnum, the great showman, bought the museum. It continued under the management of various groups in succeeding years.

February 14. Professor Samuel Morse sent a telegram to Mr. Rogers, an agent in Baltimore, that he would have to stop operations because the company appropriation was expended.

1846   The Western Continent was founded.

Grounds of the Marine Hospital were purchased for $2500.

January. The first number of the Flag of Our Union was issued.

The Bankers' Magazine and State Financial Register was published.

The Temperance Herald was first issued.

May 13. A meeting of citizens of Baltimore was held to raise volunteers to reinforce General Taylor in the war against Mexico.

May 18. Captains William Mason, Matthew Kelly, Philip M. Hale, Michael McDonald and George Baker brought an address of the Baltimore shipmasters and builders, mates and pilots to President James K. Polk asking that Baltimore be selected as a location for building warships.

May 23. A war meeting was held in Monument Square. General Samuel Houston, United States Senator from Texas, spoke to inspire volunteers.

June. The Baltimore Daily News began publication.

June 3. A company called "Baltimore's own" left by train for Washington to fight in the war against Mexico.

September 10. The New Theatre was closed by the state chancellor because of financial difficulties.

October 26. The Roman Amphitheatre was opened with the equestrian troop of Messrs. Sands, Len, and others.

1847

The Enterprise was first published.

February 4. An act of the assembly incorporated the Telegraph Company to contract and carry items on electro-magnetic telegraph invented by Samuel F.B. Morse from Washington to New York City.

March 26. The Eutaw Savings Bank was founded.

April 21. A celebration was held in honor of victories of the army and navy in Mexico.

April 29. Merchants and businessmen met at Franklin Hall to form a company to construct two steamboats for use in trade between Baltimore and Tidewater Canal at Havre-de-Grace.

June. The Bellair Market House was begun.

December 1. A meeting was held at Washington Hall for the purpose of forming an association for the promotion of the mechanical arts with Jesse Hunt, chairman.

1848

January. The Enterprise, Baltimore's first Sunday paper, was published.

February 5. The Howard Bank was incorporated.

April 9. Joseph K. Randall leased buildings and created a theater called the Howard Athenaeum and Gallery of Arts.

May 18. The first fair was held in Baltimore for exhibition and encouragement of the mechanical arts.

May 22-25. The Democratic National Convention was held in Baltimore, nominating General Lewis Cass, United States Senator from Michigan, for president and General William O. Butler of Kentucky for vice president.

May 25. The Western Telegraph line to Cumberland was opened.

May 28. A destructive fire broke out, destroying at least sixty buildings.

October 23. The Baltimore Athenaeum opened with an address by Mr. Brantz Mayer. This was a gift of the Baltimore citizens to the Maryland Historical Society.

1849

January. H.M. Garland first published the Young America.

January 10. The Greyhound, under command of Captain Claypoole, was the first ship to leave Baltimore for California because of the Gold Rush.

May. The Temperance Banner was first published by James Young.

September 17. The cornerstone for the Indigent Widowers' Asylum, being erected under the auspices of the Female Humane Impartial Society of Baltimore, was laid. The institution was dedicated on October 28, 1851.

October 1. H.M. Garland first published the *Parlor Gazette and Ladies' Advertiser*.

October 7. Edgar Allan Poe died in Baltimore.

October 30. Messrs. Martin and Company founded the *Daily City Item*.

John S. Skinner first published *The Plough, the Loom and the Anvil*.

The *Baltimore Bank Note Reporter* was founded.

1850
The population of Baltimore was 169,054.

Mr. Abbot built a rolling-mill capable of turning out the largest rolled plate in the United States. Abbot's firm was able to produce special plates of great thickness to build the *Monitor* during the Civil War.

January. Henry Mankin established a regular line of packets between Baltimore and Liverpool.

The first issue of the *Baltimore, Olio and American Medical Gazette* was published by W.C. Peters.

January 5. The first number of the *Catholic Mirror*, a weekly, was issued.

March 9. The *Weekly American* began publication.

June 29. The *Baltimore Price Current and Weekly Journal of Commerce* first appeared.

October. John Hanson was elected mayor.

December 8. Jenny Lind arrived in Baltimore. The price of tickets for her appearance was set at $3.00, but they were bid up to $100.

1851
March 5. The new Assembly Rooms were opened.

March 13. The cornerstone of the new hall for the Maryland Institute for the Promotion of the Mechanic Arts was laid. The building was opened October 20.

April 22. Archbishop Eccleston of Baltimore died at Georgetown.

May 6. The Maryland legislature incorporated the Baltimore and Potomac Railroad.

June. The United States Post Office Department rented and extended the Exchange Building.

Fall. The Baltimore Wecker, published in German, was founded by Charles Henry Schnauffer.

September. The first annual exhibition of the Maryland Horticultural Society was held in the saloon of Carroll Hall.

September 16. The Flag of Liberty, a Whig paper, began publication.

October 27. The cornerstone of the House of Refuge was laid with Governor Lowe, Chief Justice Roger B. Taney, and city officials present.

December 27. The Hungarian patriot and exile Louis Kossuth arrived.

1852

The Evening Porcupine was first published by an association of journeymen printers. It was later changed to a morning Democrat paper, the Daily Advertiser.

The American Whig was begun.

The pupils of Baltimore Female College began publication of the Parthenian or Young Ladies' Magazine.

April 26. F.K. Lipp and Company issued the first number of the Daily Times.

June 1. The Democratic National Convention opened at the hall of the Maryland Institute. It nominated General Franklin Pierce of New Hampshire as candidate for president and William R. King of Alabama for vice president on June 5.

June 10. The cornerstone of the Baltimore Orphan Asylum was laid.

June 16. The Whig National Convention met at the hall of

the Maryland Institute, nominating General Winfield Scott of New Jersey for president on the fifty-third ballot on June 21, along with William A. Graham of North Carolina for vice president.

August 21. Mills, Troxall and Company issued a weekly Whig paper the Old Defender.

September 15. Loyola College was opened. The Maryland legislature made it a University in April 1853.

October. John Smith was elected mayor

October 22. The Hanover Branch Railroad was opened.

November 13. Representatives of various Evangelical associations met at the first Presbyterian church to form the Young Men's Christian Association.

December 24. The last section of track between the Chesapeake Bay and the Ohio River was laid.

1853

The following papers and journals were founded: the Daily Republic, the American Daily Times, the Daily Globe and the Literary Bulletin.

February. John Murphy and Company issued the first number of the Metropolitan, a monthly Catholic magazine.

February 6. Messrs. Hoffman and Company issued the first number of the Sunday Morning Atlas.

March. F. Raines founded the Novellen Zeitung, an illustrated Sunday German paper.

May 18. The Fremont Savings Institution was incorporated. Its name was changed to the People's Bank on March 6, 1856.

July 14. London Park Cemetary was dedicated.

August 18. The first Know-Nothing mass meeting was held in Monument Square, with nearly 5,000 in attendance.

December. The Monumental Literary Gazette was established.

1854　　　　January. Charles F. and R.M. Cloud issued the first number of the Sunday Dispatch.

March 10. The Bank of Commerce was chartered. The Dime Savings Bank of Baltimore was also chartered.

October. Samuel Hinks was elected mayor.

1855　　　　The Baltimore Flag was founded.

January 8. The Union Protestant Infirmary was opened.

February. The first number of the Presbyterian Critic and Monthly Review appeared.

May 7. The Maryland Historical Society established a Committee on Natural History, which met every two weeks until the end of 1862.

September 10. The American Democrat was first published.

1856　　　　The Evangelical Luther and the Elevator were founded.

February. The Exchange Buildings were sold to the United States government for $267,000.

April. The first number of the Bible Times was issued.

L. Wonderman and Company founded the Leit-Storm.

September 10. The Red Men's Hall on Paca Street was dedicated.

September 17. Old Line Whigs held a national convention at the Maryland Institute and endorsed Millard Fillmore and Andrew Jackson Donelson as candidates for president and vice president of the United States.

October 8. Thomas Swann was elected mayor. Rioting occurred. The Know-Nothings used the violence to control the elections.

November 4. The national and state elections were held in which much violence ensued. The Know-Nothings were successful only in Maryland.

1857   The following papers were founded: the <u>Baltimore</u> <u>Stethescope</u>, the <u>Traveller</u>, the <u>Baltimore</u> <u>Illustrated</u> <u>Times</u> and the <u>Local</u> <u>Gazette</u>.

January 30. George Peabody, Esq., a philanthropist, was received at the Maryland Historical Society.

February 12. George Peabody established an institute for fine arts.

April 17. The first number of the <u>City Agent</u> was issued.

June 2. The first number of the <u>Monitor</u> was published by Joseph Robinson.

August 15. <u>Our</u> <u>Opinion</u> was issued by John T. Ford.

September 28. The Baltimore banks suspended specie payments.

1858   January. Mrs. Thomas Winans established a soup kitchen for the poor.

February 22. Charles J. Kerr and Thomas M. Hall published the <u>Daily</u> <u>Gazette</u>.

February 24. The general assembly incorporated the Maryland Club.

March 2. The Old Town Savings Institution was incorporated. An act of 1872 changed its name to the Old Town Bank.

March 5. Cashiers of the Baltimore banks met in the **cashiers'** room of the Union Bank, where they agreed to establish a clearing house to go into operation March 8.

March 9. The Maryland assembly incorporated the Peabody Institute and the Towsonton Railroad Company.

May 18. The first steam fire-engine in Baltimore was built for the First Baltimore Company.

June. The mayor and city council adopted the use of police and fire alarm telegraph.

September. An ordinance was passed for a paid city fire department.

September 8. A mass meeting was held in Monument Square to stop various disturbances. This led to the organization of the Reform party.

October 13. Col. Thomas Swann, Know-Nothing candidate for mayor, was reelected. Rioting occurred during elections.

1859

The following publications were founded: the Real Estate Register, the Weekly Bulletin, the Weekly Freeman, Our Newspaper, the Lily of the Valley, the American Nautical Gazette, and two German papers: Die Turn Zeitung and Zwin Zeitung.

March 14. The city council passed an ordinance granting permission to William H. Travers and others to construct a city passenger railway in Baltimore.

April 2. The first number of the Evening Star was issued.

April 16. The cornerstone of the Peabody Institute was laid.

June 27. The first operation of the police and fire alarm telegraph took place. The line was completed June 30.

July 12. The first car was on the City Passenger Railway on Broadway.

October 17. News arrived of the outbreak of a black insurrection at Harper's Ferry.

1860

January. The new jail was opened.

January 8. The Japanese ambassadors visited Baltimore.

February 2. The Maryland assembly passed a reform act appointing new police commissioners. Mayor Swann refused to hand over the police houses and equipment on February 10.

February 24. The state legislature passed an act incorporating the Baltimore, Catonsville and Ellicott's Mills Passenger Railway.

May 7. After a court fight, the old police force was disbanded.

May 8. The first issue appeared of Die Katholische Volks-Zeitung, one of the most successful Roman Catholic papers in the United States.

May 9-10. The Constitutional Union Convention, composed of the old Whig party and the American or Know-Nothing party, met in the old Presbyterian Church, and nominated John Bell for president and Edward Everett of Massachusetts for vice president.

June 12. Mayor Swann nominated commissioners to purchase sites for parks.

June 18. The Democratic National Convention, which had adjourned at Charleston, reassembled at the Baltimore Front Street Theatre. It nominated Stephen A. Douglas as its candidate for president and Senator Fitzpatrick of Alabama for vice president. When Fitzpatrick declined on June 25, the convention named Herschel V. Johnson of Georgia.

June 23. Delegates who had withdrawn from the Democratic convention met at the Maryland Institute and nominated John C. Breckinridge of Kentucky for president and Joseph Land of Oregon for vice president.

October 10. George William Brown was elected mayor.

October 19. Druid Hill Estate was formally opened as a public park.

November 26. After the election of Abraham Lincoln as president of the United States, two palmetto or South Carolina flags were unfurled as evidence of support by some Baltimoreans for the secession movement.

1861   February 1. A meeting was called to discuss the calling of a convention of the people to decide on the position of Maryland in the crisis caused by the secession movement.

February 22. President-elect Abraham Lincoln passed through Baltimore on the way to the capitol.

April 12. Baltimore received news from Charleston announcing the outbreak of war, with the firing on Fort Sumter.

April 18. Rioting occurred as a result of an attempt to transport troops from Massachusetts through the city.

April 19. A committee of citizens: Hon. H. Lennox Bond, John C. Brune, and George W. Dobbin, were sent by Mayor Brown to consult with President Lincoln about transportation of troops through Baltimore to Washington and the possible trouble which might result.

Governor Hicks consented to the burning of railroad bridges to prevent passage of troops through the city.

April 20. President Lincoln promised that no troops would pass through Baltimore if trouble were to occur.

April 20. The city council appropriated $500,000 for defense of the city.

April 22. Thomas V. Hall, Jr. issued the first number of the South, devoted to southern rights and secession. It was suppressed by the military authorities on February 17, 1862.

May 13. Troops from Massachusetts and New York took posession of Federal Hill with no resistance.

June 27. Police Marshal George P. Kane was arrested by troops and taken to Fort McHenry. The Board of Police was suspended by order of General Banks.

July 1. Police Commissioners John W. Davis, Charles D. Hinks, Charles Howard, and William Gatchell were arrested and imprisoned in Fort Warren, Boston Harbor, for over a year.

September 12-13. Mayor George Brown, various city council members and others were arrested. They were taken to Fort McHenry. John Lee Chapman, mayor ex-officio, was elected in October.

September 19. Edward F. Carter and William H. Neilson began publication of the Daily News.

October. A "wagon train" was established between Baltimore and Washington because the Potomac was closed by Confederate batteries.

December 5. The House of Refuge section for women was opened.

1862 February 13. The general assembly passed an act incorporating the Baltimore City Passenger Railway Company.

June 1. General John A. Dix was transferred from the command of Baltimore. He was succeeded by General John E. Wool.

July 8. Archbishop Francis Patrick Kenrick died.

July 28. A public meeting held in Monument Square with Governor Bradford presiding resolved to request President Lincoln to order all male citizens over eighteen to take an oath to support the Union.

October 16. J. Cloud Norris and William R. Coale published the first issue of the Sunday Telegram.

December 19. Major General Robert C. Schenck was appointed to succeed Major General Wool in command of Baltimore.

1863 January 22. At a meeting in the home of Philip Tyson, the Maryland Academy of Sciences was organized, with Tyson as president.

February. The First National Bank was incorporated.

1864 The Lyceum Observer began publication. It was the first paper published and devoted exclusively to blacks in Baltimore.

George O. Grover founded the Farmers and Planters Guide.

January. The general assembly incorporated the following companies: the Safe Deposit Company of Baltimore, the Baltimore Academy of Music, the Franklin and Powhatan Passenger Railway Company, the Baltimore, Hall's Springs and Herford Passenger Railway Company.

June 7-8. The Union National Convention met at the Front Street Theatre, nominating President Lincoln for reelection, and Andrew Johnson of Tennessee for vice president.

July 31. Martin J. Spaulding was consecrated archbishop of Baltimore.

September 5. The cornerstone of the Concordia Opera House was laid.

December 15. The Third National Bank was organized.

1865

Der Leuchtturm, a German paper, was published.

The Month, a Catholic monthly, was established.

Spring. The Douglass Institute was organized by an association of black men. Its building was opened on September 29.

April 3. Baltimore celebrated the news of General Grant's victory before Richmond.

April 6. The victory of the Union was celebrated.

April 14. President Lincoln was assassinated.

April 21. The remains of President Lincoln arrived in Baltimore. They were brought to the rotunda of the Exchange.

April 26. The cornerstone of Wildey Monument was laid.

June 5. The First National Bank of Annapolis was opened. An act of Congress in June, 1872 moved the bank to Baltimore and changed its name to the Traders' National Bank. It was opened June 1, 1874.

June 12. The Broadway Savings Bank was opened.

July. C.C. Bombaugh issued the first number of the Baltimore Underwriter.

July 31. McDonough Monument was erected by the authorities of Baltimore and New Orleans in appreciation of his contributions to the education of orphans. It was dedicated on this date.

September 20. Wildey Monument was dedicated, and a national reunion of members of the Odd Fellows was held.

The steamship <u>Somerset,</u> pioneer of the Baltimore and Liverpool Line, sailed at noon.

October 2. The first number of the <u>Baltimore Daily Commercial</u> was issued. It became an afternoon paper in 1867 and then was changed to the <u>Evening Bulletin</u> in 1869.

POST-CIVIL WAR ERA

1866

January. An extra session of the general assembly incorporated the following: the Baltimore and Savannah Steamship Company, the Union Railroad Company, the Baltimore and Havana Steamship Company and the Merchants Steamship Line.

April 2-13. The Southern Relief Fair was conducted to aid the suffering poor of the Southern states.

May 21. The Catholics of Baltimore organized St. Mary's Industrial School for Boys.

October 10. The Second Plenary Council of the Roman Catholic Church in the United States was held at the Cathedral Church.

October 25. The Peabody Institute was dedicated.

November 20. President Andrew Johnson attended the laying of the cornerstone for the new Masonic Lodge.

1867

W. Minckler and Joseph Leucht first published <u>Die Belletristischen Blaetter.</u>

January. The general assembly passed acts incorporating the following institutions: the Maryland State Agricultural and Mechanical Association, the Baltimore Warehouse Company, and the **Central** Maryland Railroad Company.

The Newsboys' Home was established.

April 10. An election was held in which the majority favored calling a convention to change the Maryland Constitution, and also to run city passenger cars on Sunday. They began running Sunday, April 28.

August. The Beneficial Savings Fund Society of Baltimore

was opened. It changed its name to the Metropolitan Savings Bank in 1876.

October. Robert T. Banks was elected mayor for a four-year term.

October 18. The cornerstone of the new city hall was laid.

November 27. The Order of the Knights of Pythias was instituted in Baltimore. Golden Lodge No. 2 and Monumental Lodge No. 2 were begun.

1868 The Knights of Crispin, one of the stronger unions with national affiliations, was organized in the city.

January. The <u>Southern Magazine,</u> a monthly, was founded by Messrs. Turnbull and Murdoch.

July 1. The German Savings Bank was chartered. The assembly changed it to a commercial bank in 1874, the German Bank of Baltimore.

November 20. The Maryland Institution for the Blind was dedicated.

January 9. The Baltimore <u>Saturday Night</u> was first issued by James H. Wood.

October 26. The first annual exhibition of the Maryland State Agricultural and Mechanical Association was held.

1870 The population of Baltimore was 267,354.

The United German Bank was incorporated as the United German Real Estate and Fire Insurance Company of Baltimore.

A law was passed prohibiting the manufacture of tin cans by convict labor.

March 1. The Central National Bank began business.

March 22. The Academy of Music was organized at the Mount Vernon Hotel, along with plans to build an opera house.

CHRONOLOGY 55

April 29. The United States Circuit Court Judge Giles ordered the Baltimore Passenger Railway Company to carry black persons on lines in the same class of cars as for other people.

August 14. The Sunday Bulletin was issued as a separate paper. Its name was changed to the Bulletin on May 11, 1871.

October 25. The Maryland Jockey Club held its first meeting at the grounds of the association at Pimlico.

November 14. An ordinance was passed for laying down tracks of the Citizen's Passenger Railway.

November 17. The Order of the Sons and Daughters of America was first introduced into Maryland and Baltimore.

November 31. The stockholders of the Baltimore Gas Light Company sold the franchises and property to New Yorkers for $3,000,000.

December 3. The first number of the weekly Our Church Work, was published.

1871   May. The German-American Bank was organized. It was incorporated in 1872.

May 1. The Union Railroad Tunnel was begun. It was completed June, 1873.

September 25. The National Commercial Convention was opened at Masonic Hall.

October. Joshua Vansant was elected mayor.

1872   The Railway World and National Economist as well as the Baltimorean were founded.

January. The first number of the monthly magazine the Amateur Journal was published.

January 23. The first grain elevator was built by the Baltimore and Ohio Railroad Company at Locust Point.

February 7. Archbishop Martin John Spaulding died.

March 30. James Anderson founded the Baltimore Dispatch.

June 8. The first number of the Baltimorean was issued.

July 9. The Democratic National Convention assembled at Ford's Opera House, nominating Horace Greely for president and B. Gratz Brown for vice president, July 10. Senator Bayard of Delaware, his delegation, and a few others were dissatisfied and held another convention at Louisville, Kentucky on September 3.

August. The Young Idea was first issued. It was edited and published by boys.

October 13. Rt. Rev. James Roosevelt Bagley was installed as archbishop.

November. The city council donated rooms over the newly built Richmond Market to the Fifth Regiment.

E.V. Hermange and Company published the first number of the Evening News.

December 14. The first number of the Enquirer, a weekly, was issued.

1873 The Baltimore News was founded.

January. Die Biene von Baltimore, a German paper, was first issued.

The first issue of the Southern Star, a monthly, appeared.

Schoolboys first published the Monthly Argus.

February 6. The new armory was formally dedicated.

March. The first number of the Baltimore Herald appeared.

March 10. Johns Hopkins sent a letter to the board of trustees indicating his designs for relief of indigent sick and orphans.

May 15. The General Assembly of the United States Presbyterian Church was opened.

May 18. The Hebrew Orphan Asylum was dedicated. William Raynor had donated the old City Almshouse, valued at $50,000.

June. The Maryland Academy of Art, through John H.B. Latrobe, president, transferred all statues, casts, etc. to the Peabody Institute.

June 22. The cornerstone of the new German Orphan Asylum was laid.

June 29. The first southern train from Richmond to use the Potomac Railroad Tunnel arrived in Baltimore.

July 17. The first issue of the People's Appeal appeared.

July 24. The first train of cars passed through the Union Railroad Tunnel from Washington to New York.

December 24. Johns Hopkins, a great benefactor of Baltimore, died. He left $6 million for the erection of a university at his country residence, Clifton, which was to include law, medical, classical, and agricultural schools as well as a free hospital for the poor of Baltimore, which would be part of the medical school, and a convalescent hospital in the country. A training school for nurses and a home for black orphans were also to be provided.

1874   The German Central Bank was incorporated.

1875   January 5. The Academy of Music was inaugurated.

April 2. The Baltimore and Potomac Tunnel was completed, making possible the junction of the Union Railroad, the Baltimore and Potomac Railroad, and the Northern Central Railroad with the Western Maryland Railroad for common use of tunnel and terminal facilities.

October. Ferdinand C. Latrobe was elected mayor.

October 3. The work of Johns Hopkins University was begun. It was the first real university in the United States.

November 17. A marble monument was erected over Edgar Allan Poe's grave.

December 23. The first issue of the Bee was issued.

1876   February 23. Daniel C. Gilman, LLD, was inaugurated president of Johns Hopkins University.

1877   The Granite Cutters Journal and the Maryland Journal were founded.

October 24. Col. George P. Kane was elected mayor.

1878   January 14. The name of the Bee was changed to the Morning Herald.

May. The first local assembly of the Knights of Labor was organized. By January 1, 1886 District Assembly 41 included sixteen local assemblies.

June 23. Mayor Kane died; a new election was required.

July 11. Ferdinand C. Latrobe, a Democrat, was again elected mayor in a special election to fill the unexpired term.

September 30. The new Peabody Library was opened.

1879   Johns Hopkins University Circulars, published monthly, was established.

October 29. Mayor Ferdinand V. Latrobe was reelected.

November 19. The Morning Herald issued an evening edition.

1880   The American Journal of Philology was established.

The following weekly papers were first published: Bayerisches Wochenblatt, Chimes, and the Manufacturers Record.

April 2. The Maryland Historical Society appointed a committee to plan the one hundred and fiftieth anniversary of Baltimore.

May 16. The Morning Herald issued a Sunday edition.

October 11-19. The one hundred and fiftieth anniversary of the founding of Baltimore was celebrated. The actual founding date of January 12, was too cold.

1881   The Charity Organization Society of Baltimore was founded to foster cooperation of various charitable agencies.

Charles Bonaparte, grandson of Jerome Bonaparte, helped form the National Civil Service Reform League, and the Civil Service Reform Association of Maryland.

The *Evangel*, a Baptist weekly, was founded.

March 25. The Maryland Savings Bank was established.

April 13. The Western Maryland Railroad was first connected with the South via the Shenandoah Valley Railroad and the Baltimore and Delta Railroad. The first train was run September 28.

May 3. The City Gas Light Company was incorporated.

May 20. The Equitable Gas Company was incorporated.

June 14. The Lady Franklin Bay Expedition, commonly known as the Greely Arctic Expedition, left Baltimore. It was led by First-Lieutenant Greely to establish meteoric and other observations within the Arctic Circle.

July 25. The stock market moved to a new site.

August 24. The Baltimore Medical College was organized.

September 25. The Hospital for Women was begun.

October 26. Ex-Senator William Pinkney was elected mayor with no opposing candidate.

1882   The *Argus*, a weekly paper, and the *American Medical Monthly* were founded.

The Federation of Labor of Baltimore was organized with thirty-two affiliated organizations.

January 22. Enoch Pratt, a Baltimore Banker, gave the city $1,083,333.33, including a building, to found a free library to be known as the Enoch Pratt Free Library, provided the city would create a perpetual annuity of $50,000 per year. This was accepted.

February 13. The <u>Baltimore</u> <u>Journal</u>, a daily German paper, was organized. A Sunday edition was added in 1885.

April. The legislature reduced the street carfare from 6 to 5 cents, and the tax on the car companies' gross receipts from 12 to 9 percent.

The Baltimore and Delta Railroad reached Towson. The first train was run in May.

July. The Thurman-Washburn-Cooky Advisory Commission was appointed to investigate the difference between the Baltimore and Ohio and the New York Central Railroads regarding rates to Baltimore. The Baltimore and Ohio's rate, which was three cents per hundred pounds less than the New York Central's rate, was announced as the acceptable one.

October 18. A mass meeting of reformers nominated William B. Stewart, a Democrat, and Charles E. Phelps and Edward Duffy, Republicans, to oppose the old judges in the election. These Independents won the election.

1883

The <u>Free</u> <u>Press</u>, a weekly paper, and the <u>Johns</u> <u>Hopkins</u> <u>University</u> <u>Studies</u> <u>in</u> <u>Historical</u> <u>and</u> <u>Political</u> <u>Science</u>, a monthly were founded.

January. Oscar Wilde visited Baltimore and delivered a lecture with little appreciation by the audience.

February. The selection of grand juries in Baltimore was transferred from the sheriff to the supreme bench.

February 19. The fire commissioners were abolished as part of a reform. J. Monroe Heiskell was appointed fire marshal in their stead.

June 1. The city began to use electric arc lights.

September. Herbert Spencer, a distinguished philosopher, visited the city.

October. The Medical College for Women was opened.

October 4. Ferdinand C. Latrobe, a Democrat, was nominated for mayor, arousing the reformers. Independent Democrats and Republicans fused to capture the city by

CHRONOLOGY 61

nominating reform candidate, J. Monroe Heiskell. Latrobe won the election.

October 12. The Baltimore <u>Sun</u> introduced the incandescent lamp to illuminate the Sun Iron Building.

October 20. The first train run over the Valley Railway reached Lexington from Baltimore.

1884 The Manual Training School was established. Soon after, it was enlarged and called the Polytechnic Institute.

The board of fire commissioners was reconstituted after a brief trial period of having a fire marshal proved unsuitable.

The <u>Golden Chain</u>, a monthly, was established.

The Bureau of Industrial Statistics was set up in response to the demands of labor unions.

1885 A new steamship line between Baltimore and Le Havre was opened.

The new Home for the Aged was opened.

The Hospital of the Good Samaritan was dedicated.

The Hotel Rennert was opened.

The <u>Maryland Churchman</u>, a monthly Episcopal journal, was established.

January. Mt. Vernon Place was adorned with a number of pieces of bronze statuary by Barye, a distinguished French sculptor. These were gifts of William T. Walters.

January 16. Henry Shirk donated a $40,000 lot on St. Paul Street for a Methodist school for girls. This was the first step in the creation of Goucher College.

August 10. The first electric railway in America went into operation on the Baltimore and Hampden Line.

October 28. James Hodges was elected mayor.

December 17. The Baltimore Oratorio Society gave its first performance.

1886

Modern Language Notes, a monthly, was established by Johns Hopkins University.

The city government began to renumber houses and also introduced a new police system.

The Real Estate Exchange was opened.

January 4. The Enoch Pratt Free Library was opened with 20,000 volumes in the main building and 3,000 in each of four branches.

April 1. The new Union Station was opened.

June 7. Archbishop James Gibbons of Baltimore Province was elevated to the cardinalate. He was the only cardinal in the United States until 1911.

August 30. The Baltimore and Ohio Railroad opened a route to New York via the Reading and Jersey Central Railroad.

September 7. The Artisans' Day celebration was held with a parade of labor organizations in Baltimore.

October 5. The cornerstone of Women's College was laid.

1887

An act of the general assembly authorized an extension of Baltimore two miles northward and one mile eastward, provided that the population in the areas agreed.

The general assembly passed an act requiring general registration every two years in Baltimore, beginning in May, 1888. It also required glass ballot boxes, and that the minority party be given representation on the Board of Supervisors of Elections.

The Daily Record was established.

March 11-12. A severe blizzard hit Baltimore and most of the eastern United States.

May 15. The people of the western and northern areas voted for annexation to Baltimore. The people of the eastern area voted against it. This area still remains part of Baltimore County.

July 1. The annexation of the western and northern areas took place; the western area became ward 21 and the northern, ward 22.

1889 Sherwood's Official Railway Guide, issued monthly, was established.

The Tablet, a Catholic journal, was first issued.

May 7. Johns Hopkins Hospital was opened. The ladies of Baltimore soon launched a movement to establish a medical school to which women should be admitted. They raised $100,000, which the university accepted, with the proviso that the total sum needed was $500,000. Miss Mary Garrett contributed the majority of the remaining sum in December, 1892.

November 5. Robert C. Davidson, a Democrat, was elected mayor.

1890 The Johns Hopkins Hospital Bulletin, a monthly, was founded.

The state legislature enacted a modified form of the Australian ballot law and provided better methods for registration.

Baltimore sold its stock in the Baltimore and Ohio Railroad and no longer had directors in its management.

John Glenn brought the National Conference of Charities and Correction to Baltimore.

The Baltimore and Ohio Railroad began construction of the Belt Line Tunnel under Howard Street, to connect Camden Station with Bayview, the southern terminus of the Philadelphia Division.

The Peabody Institute opened a music school.

The Garrett Hospital for Children was opened.

February 12. The Baltimore Sugar Refinery began operations.

May. Dr. Goucher was elected first president of the Women's College.

August 1. The first Bessemer steel was blown in Maryland at the Maryland Steel Company's works on Sparrow's Point.

August 16. The North Avenue Electric Railway began running.

October 25. The <u>World</u>, an afternoon paper, issued its first number.

November. John W. Albaugh opened the new Lyceum Theatre.

1891

The Peabody Institute accepted $90,000 left to it by the sculptor Rinehart for the promotion of art.

The new Odd Fellows hall was under construction.

The <u>Marine and Railway Gazette</u>, a monthly, was established.

The <u>Sentinel</u>, a weekly single tax paper, was founded.

May 23. One of the Cable Lines (Druid Hill Avenue) began running with the use of an underground cable. It was expensive and did not provide a smooth ride. The people finally agreed to overhead cables.

October. Ferdinand Latrobe was reelected mayor.

1892

Ladies of the Arundell Club opened a cooking school to promote the teaching of cooking in the public schools.

Alcaeus Hooper added $200,000 to the funds of the Women's College.

The <u>Afro-American</u>, a weekly paper, was established by John Murphy.

March. Druid Hill Park was adorned with a fine statue of Washington, which was formerly at Noah Walker's establishment.

The Evening News attacked the **street car companies** and advocated a state public utilities commission to regulate all utilities.

May. The <u>Evening News</u> began a series exposing frauds involved in the paving contracts.

May 28. The Baltimore and Curtis Bay Electric Railway went into service.

July 25. The Pikesville Electric Railway Line began running.

August 30. The Gilmore Street cable cars began to run.

September 17. The Central Passenger Electric Line went into operation.

October. Enoch Pratt deeded the Maryland Club property to the Maryland Academy of Sciences.

October 5-26. A General Convention of the Protestant Episcopal Church met at Emmanuel Church. It revised the Book of Common Prayer and adopted a new hymnal.

October 12. A marble statue of Christopher Columbus, presented by Italian residents in Baltimore, was unveiled in Druid Hill Park, near the lake, on the four hundredth anniversary of the discovery of America.

1893

The Charities Record, the organ of the Charity Organization Society, began to appear.

The cornerstone of the Lyric Theatre was laid.

The Johns Hopkins Medical School was opened.

The Young Women's Christian Association was opened.

The following publications were established: the Crusader, weekly; the Farmer Magazine, a monthly; the National Undewriter, a monthly; and the Standard, a monthly single tax journal.

April 23. The Lake Roland Elevated Electric Line from North Avenue was instituted.

April 26. The York Road Electric Line went into operation.

May. A commission was appointed to plan a sewage system for the city.

May 6. The Lake Roland Elevated Electric Line to city hall with Wallbrook division was running.

May 15. The Carey Street Electric Line began operating.

May 22. The "Blue Line" Cable Car Company began running. The North Avenue Electric Car Company began to operate.

July 23. Both the "Red Line" Cable Car Company and the South Baltimore Port Carey Street Electric Line began operating.

July 30. The Wilkins Avenue Electric Line, both the city and the suburban lines were opened.

August 6. The Highlandtown Electric Line went into operation.

August 20. The "White Line" Company, a street car line, began running.

September 2. The Linden Avenue Electric Line was opened.

September 3. The Maryland Avenue Electric Line, City and Suburban, began to operate.

October 4. The John Street Electric Line, City and Suburban, went into service.

November 7. Ferdinand C. Latrobe was reelected mayor. The citizens approved a $5,000,000 loan for improvements.

1894

The following publications were begun: the Atlantic Baptist, the Christian Tribune, and the Trades Unionist, all weekly papers, and the Mission Helper of the Sacred Heart, a quarterly journal.

April 2. The Citizen's Reform Association was organized.

May 31. The Baltimore Traction Company voluntarily announced free transfers, which reduced the fare from 5 cents to 3.46 cents.

1895

The following publications were established: the Jewish Comment, a weekly; the Jednota, a Moravian semimonthly; and the Poultry and Farm, a monthly.

August 1. The first of the new electric locomotives went into service on the Baltimore and Ohio Railroad.

CHRONOLOGY

November. Alcaeus Hooper was elected mayor.

1896 Two bimonthly journals were established: the Journal of Experimental Medicine and the Journal of Eye, Ear and Throat Diseases.

The Southern Fancier, a poultry monthly, was founded.

The Joint Standing Committee on Cooperation between the Charity Organization Society and the Association for Improvement of the Condition of the Poor was organized. The two groups were merged into a federation in 1902. The amalgamation was consummated in 1905 in the organization of the Federated Charities of Baltimore.

August 28. Leading members of the legal profession met at Blue Mountain House to organize the Maryland Bar Association.

1897 The following publications were first issued: the Camp Fire, a semimonthly by the Sons of America; the Catholic Monthly; the Guide, a Hebrew weekly; the National Junior, a weekly; the Postmaster, a monthly; Przyjaciel Domu, a weekly by the Polish Publishing Company, and the Southern Merchant, a monthly.

The city council passed an ordinance giving the Trustees of the Poor the power to supervise admission of patients as city charges, in order to subsidize hospitals.

April. The city hospital opened a department for the treatment of rabies by the Pasteur method.

November. William T. Malster was elected mayor. He had defeated Mayor Alcaeus Hooper in the primaries.

1898 The Ledger and the American Packer, both weeklies, along with the Patent Record, a monthly, were first published.

A law was passed by the general assembly, transferring the naming of police board members from the assembly to the governor, with the advice and consent of the Senate.

March 24. Governor Lowndes signed the Charter Act giving Baltimore a plan of municipal government.

April 25. War was declared on Spain. It had begun April 21. Governor Lowndes had called the troops of the National Guard to colors on April 24.

May 21. The Sixth Massachusetts Regiment arrived in Baltimore on the way south to war with Spain. It received a much different greeting than the group which marched through on April 19, 1861.

August 8. **Enoch Pratt's** bequest of approximately $1,250,000 to the Sheppard Asylum for the Insane became available, giving Baltimore one of the most richly endowed institutions of its kind in the world.

NEW CHARTER - HOME RULE

1899

The <u>Architects</u> <u>and</u> <u>Builders</u> <u>Journal</u>, a monthly, was established.

All brick manufacturing firms merged into the Baltimore Brick Company.

The United Electric Light and Power Company was formed **from all power companies of Baltimore.**

The United Railways and Electric Company arose from the street car lines.

April 14. Benjamin F. Newcomer stimulated local interest in the movement to eradicate tuberculosis by a gift of $10,000 for the purchase of a site for a hospital for consumptives.

May 2. A **municipal** election, the first under the new charter, was held. Thomas Hayes was elected mayor.

September 4. The Pennsylvania Railroad purchased the Baltimore, Chesapeake, and Atlantic Railway, which controlled most of the lines of steamers engaged in trade between Baltimore and the Eastern Shore tidewater region.

1900

The population of Baltimore was 508,957.

The general assembly increased the representation of Baltimore in the state legislature: from three to six in the State Senate, and from eighteen to twenty-four in the House of

Delegates. It was ratified in the November elections.

The General Oyster Law was passed because of a decline in the great packing industry in Baltimore. It regulated the issuance of licenses to dredgers and tankers, restrictions were placed on taking small oysters from beds, and inspectors and measurers were given ample powers to enforce the act.

An act was passed creating an unpaid Board of Commissioners of State Aid and Charities.

1901 February 22. The anniversary exercises of Johns Hopkins University were held. Dr. Daniel Coit Gilman announced his retirement as of September 1. His successor was to be Professor Ira Remsen, head of the chemistry department and one of the original faculty members.

October 19. The Peggy Stewart Day Monument was dedicated, celebrating the burning of a cargo of tea aboard the Peggy Stewart. It was also dedicated to Maryland soldiers who served in the War of Independence.

1902 January. An act was passed permitting women lawyers to practice in Maryland courts. Miss Ella H. Maddox, a graduate of Baltimore Law School in 1901, took the prescribed oath and was admitted to the Baltimore bar on July 9, 1902.

The legislature passed an act establishing a court in Baltimore City for trials of juvenile offenders.

January 24. The Juvenile Court, with Charles W. Heuisler as judge, was opened.

February. William Kayser, William Wyman, Samuel Keyser of New York, Francis M. Jencks, Julian LeRoy White, William H. Buckler, A.J. Ulman, and David H. Carroll donated a large tract of land in the northern suburbs of Baltimore to be part of the permanent site of Johns Hopkins University.

May 7. Baltimore's interest in the Maryland Railroad was sold to a syndicate headed by E.F. Fuller, representing the Gould and Wabash system of railroads for a total of $8,751,370.45. The bid was the lowest of four, but it was preferred by public sentiment.

July 15. The Philadelphia, Wilmington and Baltimore Railroad and the Baltimore and Potomac Railroad merged into the Philadelphia, Baltimore and Washington Railroad.

1903

April 7. The first legalized primary in Baltimore under the act of the assembly which permitted all nominations for city officers to be chosen by direct vote of people or party conventions was held.

May 5. Municipal elections were held. Robert McLane was elected mayor.

May 11. The Fifth Regiment of Infantry, Maryland National Guard, was given its new armory, built at a cost of $420,000 by the general assembly. It was good for Baltimore because it had facilities for exhibitions and great assemblies and could even draw presidential nominating committees to the city.

July. Elections for the successor to Pope Leo XIII were of interest to Baltimore because, for the first time in the history of the Roman Catholic church, an American took part in the conclave of the Sacred College. James Cardinal Gibbons, archbishop of Baltimore, attended.

1904

February 7. The great fire began in Baltimore in which 1,343 buildings burned, with 2,500 firms out of business at a loss of $125-150 million.

February 12. Mayor McLane appointed a Citizen's Emergency Committee to deal with problems caused by the fire. The city decided not to accept aid from outside because it was primarily a business problem with no dwellings affected. New quarters were taken near the center of town. This raised rents and property values greatly.

March 11. Mayor McLane constituted a board to carry out a scheme of general improvement in the burned-out area. Preliminary work was completed, including adoption of plans for wide streets, a system of docks for large coastwise steamers, and a plaza. Part of the money obtained from the sale of Baltimore's interest in the Western Maryland Railroad was used.

April 4. John D. Rockefeller, Jr., who was made aware of the losses to the hospital connected with Johns Hopkins Uni-

CHRONOLOGY 71

versity, indicated that his father would donate $500,000 to cover the hospital's losses.

May 30. Mayor McLane died as a result of a pistol bullet wound in his right temple. He had been recently married. The official verdict was suicide because of protracted nervous tension. It possibly was an accident as a result of knocking the pistol from the drawer. E. Clay Timanus, a Republican and president of the Second Branch of the City Council, became mayor.

December 5. Mayor Timanus appointed a commission, with General Felix Angus as chairman, to supervise the work of reconstruction of Centre Market, including the building of a wide thoroughfare and new dock system.

December 8. Andrew Carnegie indicated that he would donate $263,000 to the Maryland Institute so that it could erect a new building, if the city would grant the land. Michael Jenkins offered a site on Mount Royal Avenue in January, 1905. The building was dedicated on November 23, 1908 with Carnegie present.

1905

The general assembly passed an amendment to the Maryland Constitution requiring a literacy test for voting, in order to disenfranchise as many blacks as possible. It was to be submitted to a popular vote, in order to avoid the governor's veto.

February 23. The Municipal League of Baltimore was organized at a meeting at the Lyric Theatre. Among the objects of the league was an investigation of all candidates for municipal office.

July 25. The annual convention of the International Christian Endeavor Society was held in Baltimore.

November 7. Elections were held, including a vote on the constitutional amendment for a literacy test, which was defeated.

December 28. A huge floating drydock, the <u>Dewey</u>, was built at Sparrow's Point Works of the Maryland Steel Company. The dock left for its voyage of 12,000 miles to the Philippine Islands, which it successfully completed in 103 days.

1906	January. The Hayman Oyster Law was passed by the legislature, which preserved barren bottoms for private culture. A Shell Fish Commission was to be appointed by the Board of Public Works of Maryland.

An act was passed creating the Department of Legislative Reference for Baltimore City, to collect, compile, and index data for the use of municipal and state officials.

June 29. The Shell Fish Commission began field work, which was completed on November 28, 1910.

October 22. Ground was broken for the building of an extensive sewage system. The fire of 1904 had helped to increase the potential for rebuilding and improvements of this type.

1907	The Board of Trustees of Johns Hopkins University decided to admit women to post graduate courses.

May 7. J. Barry Mahool was elected mayor, defeating Mayor Timanus.

May 30-June 2. The University of Maryland celebrated its centennial.

1908	November 17. The Young Men's Christian Association building was dedicated.

1909	January 19. Baltimore participated in a nationwide celebration of the centennial anniversary of Edgar Allan Poe's birth, focusing upon a tribute to Poe at Johns Hopkins University.

November 2. Elections were held, in which an amendment to eliminate the black vote through a poll tax was defeated.

November 6. The first monument was erected by the state of Maryland in honor of Union soldiers who had fought in the war of secession. It was unveiled in Druid Hill Park. The Confederate Monument had been erected through private contributions.

1910	January. The state legislature passed a bill submitting to popular vote amendments to the state constitution enlarging the representation of Baltimore City in the legislative branch of the government.

CHRONOLOGY 73

November 6. The first aviation meeting was held in Baltimore during the week.

1911 January 13. Ferdinand C. Latrobe died. He had been mayor of Baltimore seven times.

May 16. A monument was unveiled to the memory of Francis Scott Key, author of the "Star Spangled Banner." It was the gift of Charles L. Marburg, who offered it to the city on December 15, 1906.

June 6. A celebration was held in honor of the twenty-fifth anniversary of the Cardinalate and the fiftieth anniversary of the priesthood of James, Cardinal Gibbons, Roman Catholic Archbishop of Baltimore. President William H. Taft, ex-President Theodore Roosevelt, and other national and state notables attended.

September 15. The new Union Station of the Pennsylvania and Western Railroad was opened.

October 30. The hotel Emerson was opened on the site of the historic Barnum's Hotel.

November. James H. Preston was elected mayor.

1913 June 5. The Baltimore bond sale was poor because of the stringent money market. Officials were accused of having handled the sale badly.

December 1. A New York syndicate took a loan for building sewers.

1914 February 4. The city council failed to pass a bill legalizing Sunday baseball.

May 4. City stock was sold to a syndicate of bankers.

September 5-12. The "Star-Spangled Banner" Centennial Celebration was held. Secretary of State William Jennings Bryan spoke at the closing ceremonies on September 12.

1915 May 4. Mayor Preston was reelected, along with the Democratic ticket.

1916 February 24. Baltimore was threatened with an embargo by the discontinuance of the steamship lines of the Pennsylvania Railroad under the Panama Canal Act.

May 17. Baltimore held a "Preparedness Parade."

July 7. The council passed an ordinance making it a misdemeanor to fail to stand during the singing of the "Star-Spangled Banner."

October 1. A safety-first campaign was developed by the schools and street car companies.

1917

February 18. Police Marshal Carter announced that he would ask for special guards, as a precaution against possible draft riots.

February 24-25. Mayor Preston and the board of estimate developed plans for bringing produce to the city and selling it at cost to the poor.

November 5. The concert of the Boston Symphony was banned because of a controversy over the playing of the "Star-Spangled Banner."

1918

January 12. Announcement was made that the city was prepared to advance $700,000 to the Bethlehem Steel Company to build houses for workmen at Sparrow's Point Yards.

August 26. The prices of evening newspapers were increased.

November 5. A new city charter was adopted. It provided for home rule and use of a merit system for municipal appointments.

1919

May 6. W. F. Broening, a Republican, was elected mayor.

June 2. A "wet parade" was held.

November 14. Employees of Baltimore's drydocks, and shipbuilders rose to oust Red agitators, after they called for seizure of plants.

November 27. Baltimore forbade gasoline sales on Sundays because it would be in violation of the state "blue laws."

November 30. Stores remained open as usual on Sunday although garages were closed. Many proprietors and employees were arrested, but the state attorney would not prosecute.

1920

The population of Baltimore was 733,826.

April 3. The Maryland senate passed a bill allowing Baltimore to decide whether or not Sunday showings of movies could be held.

July 7. The state Superior Court upheld a decision of the state legislature that a referendum should be held in Baltimore on Sunday moving picture shows.

August 5. The attorney general ruled that police did not possess authority to make arrests for violation of the prohibition law. The police rule was revised August 6.

August 13. J. Legum, L.B. Sless, and twenty-five others were arrested for illegal sale of whiskey.

1921

January 1. A campaign was announced to revive the prestige of Baltimore as a shipping port.

January 8. Police seized whiskey valued at $100,000.

January 24. Two thousand men mobbed the Baltimore Municipal Employment Bureau to get jobs paying thirty cents an hour.

April 22. The Merchants' National Bank of Baltimore and the National Bank of Commerce were merged.

July 8. A pay cut was announced for municipal employees.

July 25. Two thousand unemployed men answered an advertisement for thirty jobs.

August 2. The directors of the Baltimore Coal Exchange were indicted on charges of conspiring to create a monopoly in Baltimore and combining to fix prices illegally.

September 28. The Bethlehem Steel Corporation bought the Baltimore Drydock and Shipbuilding Company.

October 1. The Baltimore Highway Department adopted a part-time working plan to offset dropping employees.

October 19. Many unemployed men registered at police stations for work but refused it when it was offered.

October 20. The Edgar Allan Poe statue was unveiled.

November 23. The Baltimore police raided stores for equipment for making liquor.

1922

January 1. Mayor Broening and the city gave 2,000 unemployed citizens a New Year's feast.

May 20. The Baltimore American devised a scheme for producing purely educational films. It was endorsed by President Warren G. Harding. The first production was given at Baltimore.

June 30. Dr. M. Carey gave his Baltimore Mansion to the Baltimore Museum of Art.

1923

March 3. The Baltimore Museum presented its inaugural exhibit.

May. Mr. Jackson was elected mayor.

June 24. Baltimore housewives planned a boycott of bakers' bread in order to gain a cut in prices.

1924

January 13. The Baltimore Club dedicated its war memorial.

May 26. The United Railways and Electric Company announced a streetcar fare increase to eight cents.

July 12. St. Paul's Colored Baptist Church was stoned.

July 17. The Baltimore Federation of Labor endorsed Senator Robert Lafollette for president.

September 20. A rally was held to save Shot Tower, the oldest munitions factory in the United States.

1925

February 19. The Shelton Hotel interests purchased the armory site.

March 12. Warden Sweezy of the Maryland Penitentiary resigned after a scandal over mail order enterprises conducted by B.M. Morgan from his prison cell.

CHRONOLOGY

April 4. Show girls in Seduction were forced to wear more clothes.

April 9. Towboat operators in Baltimore struck for a wage increase.

May 11. The Circuit Court of Carroll County, Maryland, sustained the right of H. Owens, editor of the Baltimore Evening Sun, to withhold the name of the writer of a published item.

December 24. Modernists announced a plan to open an art gallery.

1926   May 17. Bonds were offered for sale for the purpose of financing municipal improvements.

May 29. The Baltimore Museum announced plans for a new building.

September 29. The Baltimore Chamber of Commerce filed a complaint with the Interstate Commerce Commission demanding a change in the freight rate differential applying on shipments from the Middle West to Atlantic ports.

1927   May 6. Baltimore issued its Metropolitan Sewer District bonds.

October 19. A planned merger of the Baltimore Copper Smelting and Rolling Company with others, to form the General Cable Corporation, was announced.

November 2. The Century Trust Company of Baltimore purchased the Storage and Trust Company.

1928   January 9. Baltimore airport bonds were issued.

January 28. The Peruvian Steamship Company announced its plan to start a new service from Baltimore to South American ports.

March 30. The Baltimore American merged with the Baltimore News.

July 7. Civic and trade groups announced work to develop harbor facilities in a race between Baltimore and New Orleans for second place in the list of American ports.

October 24. The Baltimore Bar Association refused membership to women.

November 8. The Baltimore Trust Company was appointed the Baltimore representative of the Munster and Leinster Bank.

1929

August 29. The Baltimore Palestine Legionaires volunteered to fight the Arabs.

September 12. Baltimore opened its two hundredth anniversary celebration with a parade.

November 8. The Baltimore Trust Company merged with the Century Trust Company.

1930

January 6. The United States Supreme Court allowed the United Railways and the electric company street car lines to charge a ten cent fare.

July 7. The Baltimore Mail Steamship Company was formed.

1931

February 7. The federal government gave its approval for part of the harbor development program.

April 3. The Maryland legislature passed the Blue Law Repeal Bill giving home rule to the city in the matter of Sunday closing.

May 6. Mayor H.W. Jackson was reelected.

May 9. The Baltimore Sun was awarded the University of Missouri medal of honor for distinguished service in journalism.

July 2. The City of Baltimore, flagship of the Baltimore Mail Steamship Company, sailed on its maiden voyage to Le Havre and Hamburg.

September 25. The Baltimore Mail Steamship Company added the City of Hamburg to its fleet. The City of Havre was added October 24.

1932

January 18. A $4,200,000 bond issue was subscribed in less than thirty minutes.

April 8. The Baltimore Mail Steamship Company was admitted to membership in the French Atlantic Conference.

July 8. The impending closing of the Baltimore Club was announced.

July 9. The Baltimore-Gilet Company, formed as a result of a merger of the Baltimore Trust Company and Gilet and Company, bought control of the American States Public Service Company.

September 21. The Baltimore Mail Steamship Company added Bremen as a port of call.

1933

March 24. The Baltimore Evening News bought the Baltimore Post.

April 17. The Baltimore Jewish Times published a letter from Avery Brundage, president of the American Olympic Committee, to A. Miller, indicating the possibility of transfer or cancellation of Olympic events scheduled for Berlin as a result of the Hitler government's anti-semitic attitude.

May 20. Liquidation of the Baltimore Trust Company and its replacement by the Baltimore National Bank was announced. The latter opened August 7.

September 19. Baltimore announced lottery plans to raise funds.

1935

February 9. The Baltimore Mail Steamship Line started a Baltimore to London service.

May 7. Mayor H.W. Jackson was reelected.

June 3. A Baltimore bond issue was offered. It sold for high prices on July 17.

July 9. The new name for the United railways and Electric Company was announced as the Baltimore Transit Company.

August 28. Securities of the Baltimore Transit Company were to be traded on the Baltimore Stock Exchange.

September 18. The Johns Hopkins Memorial Monument, presented by the Municipal Art Society, was dedicated.

September 30. The city council passed a resolution urging United States withdrawal from the Olympic Games.

1936   March 29. The Baltimore Mail Steamship Line announced plans to add weekly passenger and freight service from Baltimore and Hampton Roads, Virginia to London.

October 30. A statue of Martin Luther was ready for dedication.

1937   May 3. J.W. Owens of the Baltimore Sun was awarded the Pulitzer Prize for editorial writing.

May 16. The Baltimore Sun celebrated its one hundredth anniversary.

May 17. Governor Nice appointed W.P. Lawson as police commissioner to replace C.D. Gaither.

November 14. Pan American Airways began its flight service to Bermuda from Baltimore.

1938   May 27. The Baltimore Mail Steamship Company threatened to stop transatlantic operations unless its federal subsidy was increased.

June 8. The Maritime Commission authorized the Baltimore Mail Steamship Company to transfer its ships to intercoastal service.

July 9. Governor Nice refused to oust Baltimore Police Commissioner W.P. Lawson on the recommendation of the Baltimore Criminal Justice Commission in connection with his handling of bombings.

1939   March 11. Baltimore City College observed its one hundredth anniversary.

May 9. Mayor Jackson was reelected.

1940   January 4. The Maritime Commission permitted the Baltimore Mail Steamship Company to extend its New York to California service by including oriental ports.

March 19. The American Dental Association celebrated the one hundredth anniversary of the Baltimore Dental Surgery College.

	November. A sewer loan of $5,000,000 was approved by referendum. The paving referendum and daylight savings time ordinance failed.
1941	November 16. The new Municipal Airport was opened.
	December 7. Pearl Harbor was attacked. The United States entered World War ll.
1942	December 7. The Baltimore Association of Commerce gave a testimonial dinner for the British ambassador Halifax.
1943	March 10. The Balitmore Association of Commerce urged a forty-eight-hour work week for companies competing for national business.
	May 4. Theodore R. McKeldin was elected mayor, defeating Howard Jackson, who was running for a fifth term.
	May 25. The State and Electric Motor Coach Employees Association voted to strike against the Baltimore Transit Company. Violence ensued. The men returned to work June 7.
1945	May 7. M.S. Watson of the Baltimore *Sun* won the Pulitzer Prize as a war correspondent.
	August. World War ll ended.
1947	May 6. Representative Thomas D'Alesandro, Jr., a Democrat, was elected mayor.
1948	May 12. The PSC approved the issuance of Baltimore Transit Company equipment certificates to finance replacements of trolley cars.
	December 21. The Baltimore Transit Company was granted permission to raise trolley and bus fares to thirteen cents.
1949	January 19. The American and Maryland Civil Liberties Unions were permitted to intervene in contempt actions against five Baltimore stations and one commentator for alleged violation of Baltimore's criminal court code curbing crime news. The Maryland Civil Liberties Union backed the court. The ruling was challenged because it violated the freedom of the press. Judge J.B. Gray, Jr. held the four

stations in contempt on January 28. The Hearst station had been separated on January 26.

June 9. The Maryland Court of Appeals reversed the contempt ruling against three Baltimore stations and the commentator.

1950   The population of Baltimore was 949,708.

June 13. The Baltimore Chamber of Commerce opposed New York as the only northern terminal for an airline run to Puerto Rico.

December 8. Joseph H. Short, Jr., correspondent of the Baltimore Sun and Evening Sun, was sworn in as President Truman's press secretary.

1951   May 5. Thomas D'Alessandro was reelected mayor.

August 18. Police Lieutenant Ralph Amrein, the city's most decorated policeman, was dismissed for accepting a $5,000 loan from a gambler.

November 27. Police Lieutenant Sherry and ex-Lieutenant Bucher were convicted of taking bribes to allow confidence men to operate.

1952   October 8. The Pennsylvania Railroad announced plans to build a $9 million pier.

1953   January 1. A.F.L. International Teamsters struck for a twenty-five-cent hourly raise, halting various services in the city. Garbage accumulated, and the schools were closed because of lack of heat. The strike ended January 16.

September 29. Clarence W. Miles headed a syndicate that brought the American League St. Louis Browns to Baltimore as the Orioles.

1954   March 7. The Baltimore Maritime Exchange announced that it would continue in existence as a result of backing from the Steamship Trade Association.

April 15. The baseball season opened in the city. Vice President Richard Nixon attended.

CHRONOLOGY

1955 — May 3. Mayor D'Alessandro was reelected for a third term. The first black in twenty-four years was elected to the city council.

1956 — January 29. The Baltimore Coach Union went out on strike for higher pay from the Baltimore Transit Company. The men returned to work on March 6, after the state legislature passed an act barring a strike of the union. The new contract was agreed to on April 11.

December 15. Baltimore's 1957 budget of $207 million was to be balanced by a tax on manufacturers' machinery and inventory. Suits were instituted as a result of the industrial exemption granted in 1881.

1957 — May 3. The Baltimore Sunday papers raised their price from fifteen to twenty cents.

August 13. Baltimore ended the use of gas street lights.

November 15. A Baltimore ordinance was passed levying a tax on buyers and sellers of newspapers.

1958 — March 27. The city was given a plan for redevelopment of a twenty-two-acre downtown business area, costing $127 million.

May 5. J.H. Grady was elected mayor.

1960 — The population of Baltimore was 939,024.

November 2-3. The Baltimore *Sun* and *News-Post* raised prices from five to seven cents.

1962 — January 11. Canton Center, a $30 million industrial park in the port district, was planned as a complement to downtown redevelopment, which was to cost $460 million, including $113 million in federal aid.

1963 — May 7. Ex-Governor Theodore McKeldin was elected mayor.

August 29. The Baltimore City Solicitor indicated that the city was not under a constitutional compulsion to speed integration.

1964 — June 23. The city council approved a charter revision to change the administrative structure of several agencies and modernize fiscal policies.

July 25. Contracts were signed for building a theatre and a Hilton Hotel in the Charles Center urban renewal project.

September 1. Governor Tawes and Mayor McKeldin announced plans for dealing with possible black rioting at a news conference. They asked President Johnson for FBI forces on September 2.

1965

April 17. The Baltimore Sunpapers were struck. They ceased publication on April 19 when the stereotypers honored the picket lines. Picketing was extended to the affiliate television station WMAR-TV on April 21. The Sunpapers resumed publication on May 26.

1966

January 15. Mayor McKeldin asked that control of the police department, which had been held by the state since 1860, be returned to the city.

September 21. The Baltimore Orioles won the American League pennant.

October 9. The Baltimore Orioles won the World Series, defeating Los Angeles.

1967

April 18. The Inland Boatmen's Union ended a six-month strike in Baltimore. Governor Spiro Agnew had personally intervened.

September. President Fitz-roy of the Baltimore Union Stock Yards announced the closing of the organization in October because of a sharp decrease in livestock.

November 7. Thomas D'Alessandro was elected mayor, defeating Arthur Sherwood, a Republican, the first black to run for city-wide office.

1968

January 4. Ex-Mayor McKeldin was named chairman of the Baltimore Urban Coalition to tackle the problems of the poor.

January 9. Baltimore received a $22.3 million Housing and Urban Development grant for redevelopment of the city's inner harbor.

March 2. Clifford W. Mackay was named head of the Public Works Department. He was the first black bureau chief.

April 6. Governor Agnew ordered the National Guard and state police into the East Baltimore black section after rioting. Mayor D'Alessandro imposed a curfew. The White House dispatched 2,000 federal troops to Baltimore on April 7. Peace was restored on April 14.

May 13. A thirty-two-story pentagonal office tower for a World Trade Center was to be built on the waterfront as part of the inner harbor urban renewal program.

1969

January 17. The Federal Highway Administration approved a redesigned freeway plan sparing black sections.

August 9. Mrs. Helen Delich Bentley, maritime editor of the Baltimore Sunpapers was appointed a member of the Federal Maritime Commission.

September 13. The Orioles won the American League Eastern Division championship.

October 6. The Orioles won the American League playoffs and pennant. They lost the World Series on October 13 to the New York Mets.

1970

The population of Baltimore was 905,759.

January 2. Pressmen struck the Baltimore Sunpapers, which suspended publication on January 3, because most employees refused to cross the picket lines. The papers resumed publication on March 17.

June 29. The National Wildlife Federation, Sierra Club and Calvert Cliffs Coordinating Committee petitioned the Atomic Energy Commission to halt the building of an atomic plant, pending a study of the effects on the ecology of Chesapeake Bay.

DOCUMENTS

The documents in this section have been carefully selected to illustrate the rich social, political, economic, and cultural life of Baltimore from the time of its original incorporation through the 1960s. The most pertinent items from the records, ordinances, and charters of the city have been chosen, in order to give the reader an opportunity to view the changes that have come about in the development of Baltimore. In addition, specific documents pertaining to the early construction of railroads, plans for parks and thoroughfares, and the development of cultural institutions have been included in order to cover as broad a spectrum as possible. Obviously, much more could have been included, but limitations of space prevented the author from doing so. As a result, the interested student may study the complete document in the sources listed at the end of the introduction to each individual document.

ACTS CREATING BALTIMORE TOWN (1729), JONES' TOWN (1732) AND THEIR MERGER (1745)

These acts indicate the development and growth of population in each area that resulted in petitions from the residents for their incorporation as towns. Eventually the two areas had grown sufficiently to recognize the value of a merger in 1745. Specific regulations were established for purchase of the land from the original owners, dividing and surveying the lots for each town, sale to new owners, along with requirements in regard to the building of dwellings. These acts indicate the powers given to the respective commissioners and the potential for growth of Baltimore.

Source: First Records of Baltimore Town and Jones' Town. (Baltimore, 1905), pp. ix-xxiii.

An Act for erecting a Town on the North Side of Patapsco in Baltimore County; and for laying out in Lots of Sixty Acres of Land, in and about the place where one John Fleming now lives.

Whereas, several of the inhabitants of Baltimore County, have, by their Petition to this General Assembly, set forth, That a Town is much wanting on the North Side of Patapsco River; and that it is generally agreed that part of the Tract of Land, whereon a certain John Fleming now lives, and suppos'd to be the Right of the Heirs of Charles Carroll, Esq.; deceased; which said Tract is commonly Known by the Name of Cole's Harbour:

BE IT THEREFORE ENACTED, by the Right Honourable the Lord Proprietary, by and with the Advice and Consent of His Lordship's Governour, and the Upper and Lower Houses of Assembly and the authority of the same, That Mr. Thomas Talley, Mr. William Hamilton, Mr. William Bucknar, Doctor George Walker, Mr. Richard Giest, Doctor George Buchanan, Mr. William Hammond or any Three of them, shall be, and are hereby appointed Commissioners for Baltimore County aforesaid; authorized and empowered, as well to agree for the Buying and Purchasing Sixty Acres of Land out of the Tract aforesaid, and such Part, not exceeding Sixty Acres, as lies most convenient to the Water, as for surveying and Laying the same out in the most convenient Manner into Sixty equal Lots to be erected into a Town.

AND BE IT FURTHER ENACTED, That the Commissioners aforesaid, hereinbefore nominated and appointed, or the major Part of them are hereby impowered sometime before the last Day of September which shall be in the Year of our Lord God, one thousand seven hundred and thirty to meet together or the Trust aforesaid, or some other convenient place thereto; and shall then and there treat and agree with the Owner or Owners, and Persons interested in the said Sixty Acres of Land, for the same; and after Purchase thereof, shall cause the same to be so surveyed and laid out; shall cause the same Sixty Acres to be mark'd, stak'd out, and divided into convenient Streets, Lanes and Allies, as near as may be into Sixty equal Lots, mark'd by some Posts or Stakes towards the Streets, or Lanes, with Number One, Two, Three, Four and so on to Sixty, to be divided and laid out; of which Lots and Owners of the said Land shall have his or their first Choice for one Lot; and after such Choice, the remaining Lots may be taken up by others; and that no Person shall presume to purchase more than One Lot within the said Sixty Acres, during the first Four Months after laying out the same; and that the said Lots shall be purchased by the inhabitants of the County aforesaid.

And in case the said Inhabitants shall not take up the said Lots within six months after such laying out as aforesaid, it shall then be lawful for any Person or Persons whatsoever to take up the said Lot or Lots paying the Owner or Owners proportionately for the same. And in case the Owner or Owners of the aforesaid Sixty Acres of Land, shall willfully refuse to make sale of the same, or that through Nonage, Coverture, or any other disability or Impediment whatsoever, are disabled to make such sale as aforesaid, that then the Commissioners aforesaid, or the major part of them shall, and are by virtue of this Act, authorized, impowered, and required to issue Warrants under their hands and seals, to the sheriff of the said County; which said Sheriff is also hereby required and empowered upon receipt of such warrants, to impanel and return a Jury of the most substantial Freeholders, Inhabitants within the said County, to be and appear before the Said Commissioners, at a certain Day and Time by them to be limited; which Jury, upon their Oaths shall enquire to whom the said Land belongs, and assess and return what Damages and Recompense they shall think fit to be awarded to the Owners of the said Sixty Acres of Land, and all persons interested therein, according to their several and respective interests: And what sum of tobacco the said Jury shall adjudge the said Sixty Acres to be worth, shall be paid to the Owners so found by their Verdict, and all Persons they find interested therein, by such Person or Persons as shall take up the said Lots, proportionably to their Lot or Lots; which shall give the said Purchaser or Purchasers, their Heirs and assigns, an absolute Estate of Fee simple, in the said Lot or Lots; he or they complying with the Requisites in this Act mentioned.

AND BE IT FURTHER ENACTED, That the Surveyor of Baltimore County, for the Time being, shall have and receive for Surveying and Laying out the Town aforesaid the sum of Fifteen Hundred Pounds of Tobacco, and no more, to be paid and allowed him in the County Levy; and that he return a Plat thereof to the County Clerk, to be by him kept amongst the County Records. And in Case the Taker-up of such Lot or Lots, refuse and neglect to build upon such Lot or Lots within eighteen Months an House that shall cover Four Hundred square Feet; that then it shall and may be lawful for such Person or Persons whatsoever, to enter upon the said Lot or Lots, so as aforesaid not built upon, paying such sum of Tobacco as shall be first set and assessed upon such Lot to the Commissioners aforesaid or to the major Part of them, shall nominate and appoint to receive the same for the publick use and Benefit of the said Town, and to be taken up a second Time.

PROVIDED ALWAYS, That such Taker-up or Purchaser build and finish, within eighteen Months after such his Entry made, such House as in this Act is before limited and appointed to be built by the first Taker-up, which House so built, shall give and settle as good Estates to all Intents and Purposes to such second Taker-up and Builder as aforesaid, his Heirs and Assigns as is in and by this Act before limited and settled upon the first Taker-up and Builder. And in case any of the said Lots shall be neglected to be taken up in the Town aforesaid, during the Term of Seven Years next after the Publication of this Act, that then, and in such case, the Owner or Persons interested at the first in such Land, shall after such time expired, be possess'd and interested in the said Lot or Lots, as in their first and former Estate: Any Thing in this Act to the contrary notwithstanding.

AND BE IT FURTHER ENACTED by the Authority aforesaid, by and with the Advice and Consent aforesaid, That the Town aforesaid, be called by the name of Baltimore Town. . . .

AN ACT for erecting a Town or a Creek divided on the East, from the Town lately laid out in Baltimore County, called Baltimore Town, on the Land whereon Edward Fell keeps Store.

Be it Enacted, by the Right Honourable the Lord Proprietary by and with the Advice and Consent of his Lordship's Governor and the Upper and Lower Houses of Assembly and the Authority of the Same, That Mr. Thomas Sheredine, Mr. John Cockey, Mr. Robert North, Captain John Boring, and Mr. Thomas Todd, or any Three of them shall be and hereby appointed Commissioners for Baltimore County aforesaid, and are hereby authorized, and impowered, as well to agree for the buying and purchasing Ten Acres of Land out of the Tract aforesaid, and such Part, not exceeding Ten Acres, as lies most convenient to the Water, as for surveying and laying out the same, in the most convenient Manner, into Twenty equal Lots, to be erected into a Town.

And be it further Enacted, That the Commissioners aforesaid herein before nominated and appointed, or the major part of them are hereby empowered, some Time before the Thirtieth Day of November, which shall be in the Year of our Lord God, One thousand seven hundred thirty-two to meet together on the Tract of Land aforesaid, or some other convenient Place adjoining thereto, and then and there treat and agree with the Owner or Owners, and Persons interested in the said Ten Acres of Land, for the same; and after Purchase thereof, shall whereby the said Town were erected, and that the Commissioners to be appointed by this Act may have power to receive and recover the same, to be applied to the Use of the said Town; and also that the Commissioners to be appointed by this Act may have succession. They further set forth, that the several Lots in the said Towns were not taken up under the former laws, but that some have since been purchased from the Owners of said Towns; and that it is highly probable all the Lots in the said Towns, not yet taken up or purchased, in a very short Time will. Therefore they humbly pray, that such as have already purchased, or may hereafter purchase Lots within the original survey of said Towns, may to all Intents and purposes have and enjoy, as sure and indefeasible Estates in Fee-Simple, in the said Lots so purchased, or to be purchased, as if the said Lots had been taken up and improved according to the Direction of the Laws that erected the said Towns; and that all improvements, that are or may be made out of the Water, be secured to the Improver or Improvers, as fully and amply, as if the same had been originally laid out within the Bounds of the said Towns. And further they pray, that no Swine, Sheep or Geese may be kept or raised within said Town, unless kept in Inclosures. . . .

Be it therefore Enacted by the Right Honorable the Lord Proprietary, by and with the Advice and Consent of his Lordship's Governor, and the Upper and Lower Houses of the Assembly, and the Authority of the same Towns, now called Baltimore and Jone's Town, be incorporated into one entire Town, and for the future called and known by the name of Baltimore-Town, and by no other name, and that the Bridge the inhabitants of said Town have built on the Branch that divided said Towns, be for the future deemed a public Bridge, repaired and kept passable for Man, Horse, Cart, or Wagon for the future at the Expense and charge of Baltimore County.

And be it further Enacted, that Major William Hammond, Capt. Robt. North, Capt. Thomas Sheredine, Doctor George Buchanan, Col. William Hammond, Capt. Robert North, Capt. Darby Lux, Mr. Thomas Harrison, and Mr. William Fell be and are hereby appointed Commissioners, in order to see this present Act, and the former Acts relating to the Towns before mentioned, put in Execution; and that they cause the said Towns to be carefully surveyed by the Outlines of said Towns, and therein include the Branch over which the Bridge is built; and that they from time to time cause all the Lots taken up and improved, or that hereafter shall be taken up and improved, to be regularly surveyed, substantially and fairly bounded, and numbered, in order to prevent any disputes that may happen touching the Right to any of the said Lots or any part of them. . . .

ADDRESS OF ROMAN CATHOLICS TO GEORGE WASHINGTON, 1790

John Carroll, first archbishop of Baltimore and of the United States, along with other prominent Catholics wrote this letter of tribute to President George Washington congratulating him on his election to the presidency. Since this address was written after he had taken office, the Catholics were able to add a positive evaluation and praise of what his first administration had begun to accomplish.

Source: <u>The Address of the Roman Catholics to George Washington, Esq., President of the United States</u> (London, 1790.)

Sir,

We have been long impatient to testify our joy, and unbounded confidence on your being called, by an Unanimous Vote, to the first station of a country in which that unanimity could not have been obtained, without the previous merit of unexampled services, of eminent wisdom, and unblemished virtue. Our congratulations have not reached you sooner because our scattered situation prevented our communication, and the collecting of those sentiments which worried every breast. But the delay has furnished us with the opportunity, not merely of presaging the happiness to be expected under our Administration, but of bearing testimony to that which we experienced already. It is your peculiar talent, in war and in peace, to afford security to those who commit their protection into your hands. In war you shield them from the ravages of armed hostility; in peace you establish public tranquility, by the justice and moderation, not less than by the vigour of your government. By example, as well as by vigilance, you extend the influence of laws or the manners of your fellow citizens. You encourage respect for religion and inculcate, by words and actions, that principle, on which the welfare of nations so much depends that a superintending providence governs the events of the world, and watches over the conduct of men. Your exalted maxims, and unwearied attention to the moral and physical improvement of our country, have produced already the happiest effects. Under your administration, America is animated with zeal for the attainment and encouragement of useful literature. She improves her agriculture,; extends her commerce; and acquires with foreign nations a dignity unknown to her before. From these happy events, in which none can feel a warmer interest than ourselves, we derive additional pleasure, by recollecting that you, Sir, have been the principal instrument to effect so rapid a change in our political situation. This prospect of national prosperity is peculiarly pleasing to us, on another account because, whilst our country preserves her freedom and independence, we shall have a well founded title to claim from her justice, the equal rights of citizenship, as the price of our blood spilt under your eyes and of out common exertions for her defence, under your auspicious conduct -- rights rendered more dear to us by the remembrance of former hardships. When we pray for the preservation of them, where they have been granted -- and expect the full extension of them from the justice of those States (New Jersey, North Carolina, South Carolina) which still restrict them: -- when we solicit the protection of Heaven over our common country, we neither omit nor can omit recommending your preservation to the singular core of Divine Providence; because we conceive that no human beings are so available to promote the welfare of the United States, as the prolongation of your health and life in which are included the energy of your example, the wisdom of your counsels, and the persuasive eloquence of your virtues.

John Carroll, In behalf of the Roman Catholic Clergy

Charles Carroll of Carrollton,
Daniel Carroll,   In behalf of the Roman Catholic
Dominick Lynch,   Laity
Thomas Fitzsimmons

ACT CREATING CITY OF BALTIMORE
December 31, 1796

The population of Baltimore had increased greatly during the second half of the eighteenth century. The inhabitants, as well as the General Assembly of Maryland, were convinced that the affairs of Baltimore could be more efficiently handled by a city government of its own. The act incorporating the city provided for a two-branch city council and a mayor. Provisions for election were carefully indicated along with the method by which legislation could be passed and go into effect.

Source: Taken from William Kilty's "Laws of Maryland," published in 1800 in City Commissioners. Records of the City of Baltimore, 1797-1813. (Baltimore, 1906), pp. i-ix.

Chapter LXVIII

An ACT to erect Baltimore-Town in Baltimore County, into a city, and to incorporate the inhabitants thereof.

* * *

Whereas it is found by experience that the good order, health, peace and safety, of large towns and cities cannot be preserved, nor the evils and accidents to which they are subject avoided or remedied, without an internal power, competent to establish a police and regulation fitted to their particular circumstances, wants and exigencies; therefore,

II. Be it Enacted by the General Assembly of Maryland, That Baltimore-Town in Baltimore County, shall be and is hereby erected into a city by the name of The City of Baltimore, and the inhabitants thereof constituted a body politic and corporate by the name of The Mayor and City Council of Baltimore, and as such shall have perpetual succession, and by their corporate name may sue and be sued, implead or impleaded, grant, receive, and do all other acts, as natural persons, and may purchase and hold real, personal and mixed property, or dispose of the same for the benefit of the said City, and may have and use a city seal, which may be broken or altered at pleasure; the city of Baltimore shall be divided into eight wards, each ward to contain, as nearly as may be, an equal number of inhabitants; the first division shall be made by seven respectable citizens, or a majority of them, to be appointed by the governor and council; and the corporation of the said city thereafter, from time to time shall cause a correct division of the said city to be made into eight wards, according to the actual number of inhabitants, which divisions shall be repealed as after the increase or decrease of inhabitants in any ward or wards shall render it necessary in order to have a just representation, and when the inhabitants shall increase to 40,000, it shall then be divided into fifteen wards, and for any additional increase of inhabitants one new ward only shall be added for every 20,000, in order to preserve, as nearly as may be, an equal number of voters in each ward.

III. AND BE IT ENACTED, That the Council of the city of Baltimore shall consist of two branches one whereof shall be denominated The First Branch, the other The Second Branch; the first branch shall consist of two members of the most wise, sensible and discreet of the people from each ward, who shall be citizens of the United States, above 21 years of age, residents of the said town three years preceding their appointment, and assessed on the books of the assessor to the amount of $1,000; and the voters for the first branch of the said city council shall have the same qualifications as voters for delegates to the General Assembly of this State; and said elections shall be made viva voce.

IV. AND BE IT ENACTED, That the first election for members of the first branch of the city council shall be held on the third Monday in February, 1797, and on the 3rd Monday in February in each and every year thereafter, at such place in each ward as the judges of the election, in the first instance, and afterwards as the corporation by ordinance, shall direct; the election shall be held by wards, and no person shall be entitled to vote for any but the members of the ward of which he is a resident; three respectable citizens, residents in each ward, or a majority of them, in the first instance to be appointed by the Commissioners of Baltimore-Town, and afterwards by the mayor of said city, shall be judges of the elections in their respective wards, and they shall have power to appoint their respective clerks.

[By 1797, Ch. 54, the elections for members of the first branch of the city council are to be held on the first Monday in October in every year.]

V. AND BE IT ENACTED, That the polls in each ward shall be kept open one day from 8 o'clock in the morning till 6 o'clock at night, and no longer, and when closed, the several judges shall, within three days after such election, notify to the persons having the greatest number of legal votes in their respective wards that they are duly elected; . . . any vacancy happening in the first branch of the city council shall be filled up without delay from the ward where such vacancy happened in such manner as shall be hereafter directed by ordinance.

VI. AND BE IT FURTHER ENACTED. That the Second Branch shall consist of eight members, who shall be chosen from the several wards, and no person shall be eligible as a member of the second branch, who is not of the full age of twenty-five years, a citizen of the United States, and a resident of the said town four years previous to his election, and assessed on the books of the assessor to the amount of $2,000, and the members of the second branch shall continue in office for a term of two years next succeeding the time of their election.

VII. AND BE IT ENACTED. That the Mayor of the said city, and the members of the second branch of the city council shall be chosen in the following manner, to wit: That each ward, at the time and place of electing the first branch of the city council, shall elect <u>viva voce,</u> one person qualified to be a member of the first branch as elector of the mayor and of the members of the second branch of the city council, on the third Monday in January next, and on the same day in every second year thereafter, (a) who shall, on the third Monday of February, 1797, and on the same day every second year thereafter, meet at the court-house or some other convenient place on the said city, and elect by ballot, a mayor and eight members of the second branch, to serve for two years thereafter; no person shall be eligible for mayor who is not of known integrity, experience, and sound judgment, 25 years of age, ten years a citizen of the United States, and five years a resident of Baltimore-town, or city, next preceding the election; and in case two or more persons shall have an equal number of votes for mayor, or members of the second branch, the said electors shall determine by lot, which of the persons having an equal number of votes, shall be appointed to the office of mayor, or second branch of the city council, as the case may require the said electors of the mayor and of the members of the second branch, before they proceed to elect, shall swear or affirm, as the case may be, that they will elect, without favor, partiality or prejudice, such person for mayor, and such persons as members of the second branch of the city council as in their judgment and conscience believe best qualified for the said offices, and having the other qualifications required by this act; that the said electors shall be judges of the elections, returns and qualifications of their members, but no person shall be elector of the mayor and member of the first branch of the city council at the same time; any vacancy happening in the electors of the mayor shall be filled up from the ward where such vacancy happened, without delay, . . .

DESCRIPTION OF BALTIMORE, 1799

Col. J. Thomas Scharf presented the following newspaper description of the Baltimore of 1799 in his Chronicles of Baltimore. It indicates that the City was a growing and prosperous one, which had in fact shown a great deal of ability to take advantage of its location and opportunities.

Source: J. Thomas Scharf. The Chronicles of Baltimore; . . . (Baltimore, 1874), pp. 288-289.

"Baltimore, the largest and most flourishing commercial city in the State of Maryland, is situated in a county of its own name, and on the N.W. branch of Patapsco river. It extends from Harris's creek on the S.E., until it reaches a branch of the western branch, over which there are three wooden bridges. In the city the streets extend from east to west, along the north side of the basin, and these are again intersected by others at right angles, extending north from it; except a few which run in different directions. At Fell's Point the streets also in general extend from east to west, and are crossed by others at right angles; but immediately on the Point there are a few which run in various directions, as circumstances would admit of. On the side Jones Falls, there are some which extend parallel to it, and vary their course from the former. The number of streets, lanes and alleys, is about 130; but several of these are yet without a building. The buildings are principally placed between Howard street and the Falls. The main street is 80 feet wide, and extends from east to west about three-quarters of a mile, and is called Baltimore street. Pratt, Water, Second and East street (Fayette) have the same direction, and are from 40 to 60 feet wide. These are intersected at right angles by Market street, 150 feet wide, Frederick, Gay, South, Calvert, Charles, Hanover, and Howard streets, which are from 66 to 80 feet wide, and compactly built. There are others partly built, as Holliday street 100 feet wide, where the new theatre stands, Lovely and St. Paul's lanes thirty feet wide, &c. The public buildings are a court-house, jail, market-houses, a poorhouse, which stands on the northwest side of the town, besides three banks and exchange, and a theatre already mentioned: these last are private property. The Bank of Maryland stands in South street, between Walnut street and Lovely lane, and was incorporated in 1791; its capital is $300,000. The branch Bank of the United States stands at the corner of Second and South Gay streets. The Baltimore Bank stands in Baltimore street -- No. 154. The court-house is a brick building erected upon an arch in the north end of Calvert street. In the next square, a little to the northwest, is the jail (now record-office). The houses for public worship are eleven, viz: one for Episcopalians, one for Presbyterians, one for German Lutherans, one for German Calvinists, one for the Reformed Germans, one for Nicolites or New Quakers, one for Baptists, one for Roman Catholics, and two for Methodists, one of which stands at Fell's Point. The Presbyterian church stands in East street (northwest corner of North and Fayette streets), has a handsome portico, and is supported by six pillars in front. It is well-finished, and is one of the most elegant churches in America. The houses as numbered in 1787 were 1955; about 1200 of these were in the town and the rest at Fell's Point. The number of houses at present is about 3500: the greater part of these are brick, and many of them handsome and elegant. The number of warehouses is about 170, chiefly placed contiguous to the harbor; and the number of inhabitants, according to the census taken in 1791, was 13,758, of whom 1255 were slaves; but this must be far short of the present number.

"The basin is on the south side of the town, in which the water at common tides is from eight to nine feet deep. The harbor at Fell's Point is deep enough to admit ships of 500 tons burthen. The situation of part of the town is low, and was unhealthy until a large marsh was reclaimed about twenty-seven years ago, since which time the town has been as healthy as any other in the United States. Where the marsh formerly was there is a market space 150 feet wide, which we have mentioned above; on each side is a row of buildings, with the market-house in the centre. Perhaps the increase of houses, and consequently of smoke, together with the improvements which have been made in paving the streets and keeping them clean, may also have contributed in rendering it so healthy. The articles manufactured here are sugar, rum, tobacco, snuff, cordage, paper, wool and cotton-cards, nails, saddles, boots, shoes, ship-building in all its various branches, besides a variety of other articles. Within eighteen miles of the town there are fifty capital merchant-mills, one powder-mill, and two paper-mills, besides several furnaces and two forges. Twelve of the merchant-mills are within four miles of the town, on Jones Falls, and four others are about the same distance on two other streams. Adjoining the town is a large mill, with four pairs of stones six feet in diameter, capable of manufacturing 150 barrels of flour in a day; the water-course is about a mile in length, one-third part of which is cut out of solid rock: in this distance the water gains sixty-five feet fall. The rapid increase of Baltimore has even surprised its friends, and it now ranks as the third commercial port in the Union. There were belonging to it in 1790, 27 ships, 1 scow, 31 brigantines, 34 schooners, and 9 sloops: total 102 vessels, containing 13,564 tons. In the year ending the last day of December, 1797, the shipping amounted to 59,837 tons. The exports in 1790 amounted to $2,027,770, and the imports to $1,945,899; balance in favor of Baltimore, $81,971. In the year ending September, 1794, the exports amounted to $5,094,248, and in 1798 ending September 30th, $12,000,000 and upwards. . . .

BY-LAWS FOR THE GOVERNMENT OF THE POOR, 1826

> Provisions were made for the establishment of an Alms House, including the Board of Trustees, the Agent and Matron, as well as medical attendance for the poor. Provisions were made for the constant medical attention of the poor by medical students who were to report to the Physician in charge.

Source: <u>By-Laws for the Government of the Poor, and Poor House of Baltimore City and County, 1826</u> (Baltimore, 1826.)

At a meeting of the Trustees for the Poor of Baltimore City and County, on Monday, the ninth day of January, in the year 1826, the following,

BY-LAWS,

for the Regulation and Government of the Poor House or Alms House, of Baltimore City and County, of the officers thereof, and of the persons therewith connected and therein contained and employed, were unanimously adopted.

The Trustees

1. At the first meeting of the Trustees after their appointment, they shall annually elect from amongst themselves a President, Treasurer, and Secretary to the Board; and an Overseer, Physican, Agent, and Matron, shall be appointed on the first Monday in May in every year.

* * *

4. The Trustees shall meet very Monday at 10 o'clock, A.M. alternately at the Alms House and at the office of the Agent in the City of Baltimore.

5. Weekly visits shall be made by one of the Trustees in rotation, to examine into the state of the Alms House, and of the Poor, and such other matters as may require inspection; and such visiting Trustee shall report to the Board at its next weekly meeting.

* * *

8. No spiritous liquors nor other drink, except water, shall be used at the table of the Alms House, nor shall any spiritous liquors or other drink, except water, be upon any pretext whatever furnished to any person

resident in or attached to the establishment, except when prescribed by one of the physicians as medicine, in which cases it shall be supplied from the Hospital department.

* * *

The Poor.

21. Every person admitted into the Poor House, for support, shall on arrival, inform the overseer of his or her name, age, occupation, disease and place of nativity, and shall forthwith be examined by the overseer or matron, and washed and changed if it should be thought necessary. . . .

* * *

The Sick.

34. It shall be the duty of the Physician, to see that the persons admitted into the house in ill health, be cleansed and changed, as far as may be consistent with their safety, and to designate the sick rooms in which they shall be placed.

35. When the life of a patient is in immediate danger, he or she shall be kept as undisturbed as possible, and when death ensues, the corpse shall forthwith be put into a coffin, and removed to the apartment prepared for the dead.

36. It shall be the duty of the overseer to see that the interment of the dead shall not take place in less than twelve hours in summer, and twenty-four hours in winter, after their decease, unless especially required by the nature of the disease, or the state of the corpse, which shall remain until interment, subject to the view of friends or orderly visitors, who may desire to see it.

The Children.

37. The children shall have careful and competent nurses and teachers selected by the overseer, and shall be constantly supplied with school books and Testaments; and when over six years of age, the sexes shall be lodged separately.

38. A school shall be kept in the house, and the children be daily taught reading, writing, and arithmetic. They shall be bound out apprentices to persons well known to the Trustees, or to such as may be suitably recommended to them. A duplicate of the indentures, stating the residence of the masters or mistresses, shall be kept by the overseer for the inspection of the Trustees and of those interested.

* * *

84. The farmer shall keep a book in which he shall enter the names of all persons in his employ, also stating when they commenced to labour with him, and noting at the time when they may absent themselves, or not work, . . .

Medical Department.

85. The Officers of the Medical Department, shall consist of an attending Physician and as many students of Medicine as the Trustees of the Institution may deem expedient.

86. The attending Physician shall visit the Alms House at least once a day, and oftener should there be a necessity for his services.

* * *

90. It shall be the duty of the attending Physician to be present at all important operations of surgery, which it may be necessary to perform in the institution, and if he does not operate himself, to assign the cases to the students in the following order, The Obstetrick cases alternately, commencing with the senior student, and in such cases, not more than two of the students shall be in the room at the same time -- in difficult cases, and especially in such as require artificial aid; the physician shall direct the procedure in the presence of all the students. The surgical operations of all other kinds shall if relinquished by the physician, as abovementioned, be assigned to the students alternately, if of the same class -- but the first of each class . . . may be claimed by the senior student.

91. The student who shall have resided for the longest period in the house, shall be denominated the senior student, provided he shall be deemed competent by the attending physician -- all the students shall be accomodated in the house, with boarding, lodging and washing, and shall each pay to the agent of the Trustees for his accomodation the sum of Two hundred dollars per annum, half yearly in advance, the payment of which sum in advance shall be an indispensable requisite, but after a student shall have paid $400 for the first two years he may remain and enjoy all the advantages of the institution the third year free from expense.

92. The students shall be under the direction of the attending Physician, who shall take charge of their medical education, assign to them their various duties in the medical department, and be responsible to the Trustees for the faithful discharge of those duties as well as for their care and deportment whilst they remain in the institution . . . .

RECOMMENDATIONS FOR THE ERECTION OF THE BALTIMORE AND OHIO RAILROAD, 1827

The merchants of Baltimore became very much concerned over the effects of the Erie Canal on the prosperity of the city as more and more trade went to New York City. Consequently, a thorough study was made of the future value of canal and railroad transportation in the carrying of freight. The study concluded that the railroads would be the mode of transportation of the future, and the construction of the Baltimore and Ohio railroad was recommended for immediate consideration and development.

Source: Baltimore. Citizens. <u>Proceedings of Sundry Citizens of Baltimore, Convened for the Purpose of Devising the Most Efficient Means of Improving the Intercourse Between that City and the Western States (Baltimore, 1827.)</u>

Baltimore, February 12, 1827.

At a meeting of a number of Citizens to take into consideration the best means of restoring to the City of Baltimore that Portion of the Western Trade which has lately been diverted from it by the introduction of Steam navigation, and by other causes, William Patterson, Esq. was appointed chairman, and David Winchester, Secretary.

Various documents and statements, illustrating the efficiency of Rail Roads, for the conveying of articles of heavy carriage, at a small expense, were produced and examined; and the superior advantage of this mode of Transportation, over Turnpike roads or Canals, in many situations being, according to those statements, satisfactorily shown, it was on motion, Resolved that the said documents be referred to a Committee whose duty it shall be to examine the same, together with such other facts and experiments as they may be able to collect; and when prepared, to report their opinion thereon, and on the course it may be deemed proper for this meeting to pursue.

Report

Whilst the cities of Philadelphia and New York are making such great and efficient exertions to draw to themselves the trade of the West, it cannot be expected but that Baltimore must soon lose the comparatively small portion which remains to her of this trade, should she continue inactive, and not avail herself of the great and decided advantages her local situation gives to her. The effort now making to connect the Tide water of the Susquehanna by means of a canal navigation with the Eastern extremity of the Pennsylvania State Canal, it is confidently hoped, by the friends of that measure, will secure to us the ascending and descending trade of this noble river, and perhaps will lead hereafter to a direct water communication with the great northern lakes, with whose tributary streams the Susquehanna interlocks. In completing this measure we shall therefore do all that we are now called upon to execute in reference to the River Susquehanna.

But important as this Trade is to Baltimore, it is certainly of minor consideration, when compared to the immense commerce which lies within our grasp to the West, provided we have the enterprise to profit by the advantages which our local situation gives us in reference to that Trade. Baltimore lies 200 miles nearer to the navigable waters of the West than New York, and about 100 miles nearer to them than Philadelphia, to which may be added the important fact, that the easiest, and by far the most practicable route through the ridges of Mountains which divide the Atlantic from the Western waters, is along the depression formed by the Potomac in its passage through them. -- Taking then into the estimate, the advantages which these important circumstances afford to Baltimore, in regard to this immense Trade, we again repeat that nothing is wanted to secure a great portion of it to our City, but a faithful application of the means within our power.

The only point from which we have anything to apprehend, is New Orleans: with that city, it is admitted we must be content to share this trade because she will always enjoy a certain portion of it in defiance of our efforts; but from a Country of such vast extent, and whose productions are so various and of such incalculable amount, there will be a sufficient Trade to sustain both New Orleans and Baltimore; and we may feel fully contented if we can succeed in securing to ourselves that portion of it which will prefer to seek a Market East of the Mountains.

Of the several artificial means which human ingenuity and industry have derived to open easy and economical communications between distant points, Turnpike roads, Canals and Rail Roads, have unquestionably the advantage over all others: when Turnpike roads were first attempted in England, they were almost universally opposed by the great body of the people, a few enterprising citizens however succeeded after a severe struggle in constructing them. -- The amount of travelling was then so limited, that this means of transportation was found abundantly sufficient for all the exigencies of the then trade of that country; in a little time however, so great was the increase of commerce there, (and which increase in a great measure resulted from the advantages these roads afforded) that even, the Turnpikes in a short time were found insufficient to accomodate the growing Trade of the Country, and the substitution of Canals in the place of Roads was the consequence, in every situation where the construction of them was practicable.

It was soon ascertained, that in proportion to the increased facilities afforded to Trade by the Canals in England, was the increase of Trade itself, until even this means of communication was actually in many of the more commercial parts of the Country, found insufficient for the transportation required.

Rail Roads had, upon a limited scale, been used in several places in England and Wales for a number of years. and had, in every instance, been found fully to answer the purposes required, as far as the experiment had been made. The idea applying them upon a more extended scale, appears however only recently to have been suggested in that Country, but notwithstanding so little time has elapsed since the attempt was first made, yet we find that so decided have been their advantages over Turnpike Roads, and even over Canals, that already 2,000 miles of them are actually completed in a train of rapid progress, in Great Britain, and that the experiment of their construction has not in one case failed nor has there been one instance in which they have not fully answered the most sanguine expectations of their projectors. Indeed, so completely has this improvement succeeded in England, that these roads will, for heavy transport, supersede Canals as effectually as Canals have superseded Turnpike roads.

[Report then discusses advantages which Canal system has in England which it does not have in the United States.]

. . . There has yet in this country, been but one Rail Road constructed and fully tested, and this is only about three miles long; it cost $11,000 per mile, but it is alleged that with the experience now gained, a similar one could be constructed for about one-third less. We here refer to the Quincy Rail Road near to Boston; it was erected as an experiment, and as far as it has been tried, has fully answered the expectations of the parties for whose use it was made; not having been the least injured by the severe frosts during the late winter. The stock of information upon the general subject of Rail Roads, now in possession of this Committee is admitted not to be very extensive, but they have gleaned from the several publications and reports which they have examined upon this interesting subject, enough to leave no doubt upon their minds, that these roads are far better adapted to our situation and circumstances, recommend that measures be taken to construct a double Rail Road between the City of Baltimore and some suitable point on the Ohio River, by the most eligible and direct route, and that a charter to incorporate a Company to execute this work be obtained as early as possible; . . .

RECOMMENDATION FOR A RAIL ROAD
FROM BALTIMORE TO THE SUSQUEHANNA RIVER, 1827

The construction of the Erie Canal by New York State helped to raise New York City to great prosperity. Both Baltimore and Philadelphia were very much threatened. As a result businessmen in both cities were very much interested in promoting the development of rival canal systems. Residents of Baltimore came to the conclusion in 1827 that the construction of a railroad would be much more beneficial in recapturing some of the lost trade from the Middle West. Consequently various canal and turnpike companies came together to study the situation and recommended the erection of a railroad from Baltimore to the Susquehanna.

Source: Report and Proceedings in Relation to a Rail Road from Baltimore to the Susquehanna (Baltimore, 1828.)

Baltimore, August 3rd, 1827.

On this day, a meeting consisting of delegates from the Baltimore and York Turnpike -- the York and Maryland -- the Conewago Canal Turnpike, and the York Haven Company, was held in the city of Baltimore, in the Exchange buildings, when JOHN SMITH HOLLINS was called to the Chair, and George Winchester appointed Secretary.

On motion, the following resolutions were adopted: --

Resolved, That in the opinion of the delegates here assembled, it is desirable that a survey or examination of the country between Baltimore and York Haven should be made by a Committee to consist of at least one delegate from each of the incorporated companies here represented, with a view to obtain such information, to be communicated to the several turnpike companies, as will enable them to decide whether it be practicable to make a rail-road upon the bed of the present turnpike, or whether it will be advisable for them to unite in constructing a rail-road from Baltimore to York Haven; and that the several corporations here represented contribute equally, to the expense of such an examination.

Resolved, That the Committee unite with the gentlemen appointed at York Town for the purpose of making the survey and the secretary is directed to notify them of the proceedings of this meeting, and request their attendance in Baltimore.

In pursuance of the above resolutions and proceedings, a committee was appointed and proceeded, during the month of August last, to make the investigation directed.

Their report . . . is now submitted to the consideration of the people of Baltimore.

It has been delayed until this moment, that no room should be left even for conjecture that the project which it represents was intended, or should in any manner, interfere with the great scheme of the Baltimore and Ohio rail-road. Public opinion is now so settled as to the importance and feasibility of that enterprise, as to place it beyond the reach of competition, and far above the opposition or impediment from any quarter, even if such were intended. It is believed by those who are instrumental in bringing before the public the Susquehanna rail-road, that it will by its success, tend to strengthen public opinion and sustain the confidence of the community in the magnificent undertaking which has preceded it.

To the President and Directors of the York Road, the York and Maryland Line Road and Conewago Canal Turnpike Road, and the York Haven Company.

The Committee appointed by a Convention of Delegates from the above institutions, to examine into the practicability of making a rail-road line from Baltimore to the Susquehanna, now report --

That in execution of the object of their appointment, a majority of the committee proceeded to examine and explore the country between Baltimore and the Susquehanna, with a view to obtain the information requisite to a judicious direction of such future operations as might grow out of the suggested enterprise of a railroad from Baltimore to the Susquehanna.

The more immediate object of their appointment, the committee are well aware, was to ascertain the practicability of making a rail-road upon the bed of the present turnpike road, commencing at Baltimore, passing by Yorktown and terminating at York Haven, upon the Susquehanna. To this particular object the Committee have not failed to pay the proper and necessary attention; but the pursuit of that investigation, extended their views over a more enlarged field of enquiry to the general question of the practicability of a rail-road from Baltimore to the Susquehanna, without reference to any previously designated route -- indeed the special object of their appointment necessarily called for this enlarged examination of the country adjacent to the line of the turnpike road, inasmuch as the positive advantage of it with other routes, which the reconnaisance of the country necessarily brought under the inspection of the committee . . . .

The public mind has at length become directed to the improvement of our internal resources, and it is a matter of great gratification to find the sentiment pervading the whole community, that the commercial existence of the city, rests upon opening an intercourse with the vast regions west of the Alleghany, and the extensive tracts of country included within the states of New-York, Pennsylvania, and Virginia. To facilitate the natural means, or to create an artificial easy means of communication with this immense region seems now to occupy the undivided public opinion -- the liberal and enlightened -- the bold and manly enterprise which belongs to our city, is all directed to the completion of this magnificent undertaking, and we may look forward with a well founded confidence to the period, when we shall realize all its promised reward.

That the period for systematic and powerful exertion on the part of Baltimore has at length arrived, is no longer doubted -- the great plans which are going on and in a great measure matured in New-York, and those which are projected and will be completed in Pennsylvania, show a determination on the part of our rival cities to push as far as unlimited capital, seconded by liberal views and great enterprise, a compensation, which can only become dangerous, if we permit their schemes to be matured, and the current of the race to take a settled direction in the channels provided for it by our rivals -- for commerce like water will seek its level, depending on natural or artificial causes, and if we once permit it to be diverted from its natural channel it will be found most difficult to bring it back. If on the other hand we enter early into the field of competition, and improve our natural advantages, we make the efforts of our rivals tributary to our views, and they cannot make a foot of canal on rail-way, erect a bridge, or pave a turnpike road, which does not necessarily head the trade or commerce embarked upon it directly to our door. We have nothing in fact to do but to take up the work where they leave it, and to finish at a trifling expense a great line of internal communication, which the exertions of our spirited and enterprising neighbours have conducted within our reach.

* * *

The trade of the Susquehanna which now floats on the surface of the river and finds its way through this natural channel to Baltimore, will, when the system of canals shall be completed in Philadelphia, be carried to a market through the artificial communications thus provided: and it is manifest therefore if we expect to retain the trade of that country, we must secure it by means of roads and canals, similar to those which our neighbours are making to conduct it to their capital.

The moment for commencing this system has, as all agree, at length arrived, and the only question now remaining is not whether it shall be done, but what is the best mode in which it can be done.

The division of public opinion on the subject of a canal for the Susquehanna has retarded the progress of this important communication for many years, but it seems now to be a general, and indeed almost a universal impression that a rail-road from Baltimore to the Susquehanna presents the cheapest and best mode of forming this important communication, and to examine and ascertain the correctness of this opinion was the duty committed to our charge, . . . we trust it will produce conviction in the truth of our general views, and an accordance in the opinion which we entertain that a rail-road from Baltimore to the Susquehanna is practicable at a moderate expense, and will afford an ample revenue for the capital wanted in its construction.

BY-LAWS OF THE BOARD OF TRADE OF BALTIMORE,
Adopted 1849

The growth of business firms in Baltimore had reached a stage where it was found necessary to form a Board of Trade which could regularize relationships among the many organizations in the City. In addition, the many problems which eventually developed into litigation before the law courts were recognized as a deterrent to the normal flow of business. Therefore the Board of Trade provided for a Court of Arbitration which would provide for a better means of settling disputes.

Source: Baltimore Board of Trade. Constitution and By-Laws adopted 1849. Act of Incorporation Passed Maryland Assembly, May, 1852, with Amendment to Same, Passed 1878, Providing for a Court of Arbitration, Together with Rules Governing Said Court, Adopted by the Board of Trade, July, 1878. (Baltimore, 1878).

Preamble

Believing in the necessity of an association of citizens to give tone and energy to their efforts in securing the advantages which the position of the city offers to Commerce and Manufactures and that this end may be accomplished by the establishment of a BOARD OF TRADE, the duty of whose Executive shall be to consider all subjects of internal improvement agitated in the same community, which may be brought under their notice by members of the same and take such effectual measures in relation there to as the importance of the subject shall call for; to settle and adjust all matters relating to the trade of the city; to establish its customs and ordinances, and to maintain unity of action for public good: We hereunto subscribe to the following articles of association.

ARTICLE OF ASSOCIATION
of the
BOARD OF TRADE OF THE CITY OF BALTIMORE.

Article 1. The officers of this "Board of Trade" shall consist of a President, four Vice-Presidents, twenty-four Directors, a Secretary, and a Treasurer, who shall be chosen by ballot, annually, at the annual meeting. And the Secretary shall be remunerated for his services by such salary as may be fixed by the President and Directors annually.

Art. 2. This Association shall hold annual and special meetings. The annual meeting shall be held on the first Monday in October of every year, and special meetings may be called by order of the President, or one of the Vice-Presidents, when occasion may require, of which the Secretary shall give public notice.

Art. 3. The Board of Directors shall meet statedly, on the first Monday of every month, for the transaction of such business as may come before them; and at the stated meeting in October, shall lay before the Association a report of the proceedings of the past year. . . .

Art. 5. The said officers shall appoint a standing Monthly Committee, consisting of five members of the Association, which shall be styled the Committee of Arbitration, (two of whom shall be rejected by the litigants.)

Art. 6. The duties of the Committee of Arbitration shall be to arbitrate and decide all disputed accounts and contracts, and all controversies of a mercantile character, which may be brought before them by the members; the parties having previously signed a Penalty Bond, for such an amount as the Committee may require, to abide by the decision of the same.

Art. 7. The Committee of Arbitration shall render their awards in writing to the parties in controversy, through the Secretary of the Board, within one week after their decision shall have been made. . . .

Art. 11. No member of the Association, who is cognizant of any fact or facts in a case before the Committee of Arbitration, shall refuse to give testimony before said Committee, if notified in writing by the Secretary, of the time and place, when and where his evidence may be required, upon pain of expulsion from the Association, without a satisfactory excuse for such a refusal.

Art. 12. The Secretary shall keep an accurate record of the transactions of the Board of Directors at their monthly meetings, and of the annual meetings of the members, attend the sittings of the Committee of Arbitration, record their decisions, give notice to said Committee when their services are required, render a copy of their verdicts to the parties in the case, collect the fees of arbitration, and all other monies due the Board, and pay the same over to the Treasurer, read the minutes of the last previous meeting at the monthly meetings of the Directors and annual meetings of the members, and report the proceedings of the Committee of Arbitration at each meeting of the Board of Directors.

Art. 13. The Treasurer shall receive from the Secretary all monies belonging to the Board, shall disburse the same when approved by the President, or one of the Vice-Presidents, and shall report the receipts, expenditures, &c., at each monthly meeting of the Board and annual meeting of the Association.

Art. 14. The funds of the Association shall always be subject to the control of the Board of Directors, but they shall have no power or authority to enter into any contract binding on the members of the Association, beyond the funds in the hands of the Treasurer.

Art. 15. Any individuals or firms (residents of Baltimore,) may become members of this Association, on the payment of three dollars per annum, payable in advance which shall become due on the first Monday in October, said firms to have but one vote; and any neglect or refusal to pay said contribution for one year, shall be considered as a withdrawal from the Association, and the name of the party shall be stricken from the same.

Art. 16. The Board of Directors shall have power to make such By-Laws as they may deem necessary; to fill any vacancy occurring among the officers; and to alter or amend these articles of association, provided a majority of three-fourths of all the members of the same is obtained in favor of said alteration, at an extra meeting to be called for the purpose, by order of the President, of which the Secretary shall give each member of the Board notice.

The Court of Arbitration of the Board of Trade of the City of Baltimore

The practice of settling the controversies which arise between individuals, touching their civil rights and the violation of these, by <u>arbitration,</u> has always been and everywhere in favor. Where men honestly differ in this regard, and cannot themselves compose their differences, the next resort naturally is to the intervention of impartial friends whose judgments unbiased by any personal interest, may determine what is right and just to be done in the particular instance, and do for the parties what they cannot accomplish for themselves. Only when this expedient has, upon trial, proven inadequate to a satisfactory settlement of their dispute, will those who <u>honestly differ</u> need to have recourse to the expensive and dilatory process of litigation in the public courts. The whole community bring the controversies arising in the daily transactions of business to these tribunals for adjustment; their dockets are therefore crowded; each litigant must take his turn in the always extended succession of suitors; the general rules which must necessarily be established for the regular and orderly despatch of business, and one, in general, effectual to this end, will yet, from their uniformity and inflexibility, often, in special individual cases, made exceptional by the existence of elements which the rule does not recognize or provide for, defeat justice, -- and so delay and sometimes actual injustice result.

Arbitration has always been a favorite mode among <u>merchants</u> and <u>business men</u>, more perhaps than any other class, of reconciling and composing differences arising in the prosecution of their business operations, and the collision and conflict of the interests involved in these.

"Cases of misunderstanding and disagreement continually occur in the immense mass of transactions which make up each day's trade. When these are carried into the ordinary courts the expenses are very great and the time consumed often counted by years. When at last the trial shall have been reached, witnesses may be dead or scattered, and claims that ought to have been recovered are thus abandoned or lost." And even if the <u>issue</u>

of the litigation be more favorable, yet the uncertainty, during the long suspension of final determination, may and often does seriously embarrass and cripple the business operations of the parties or of one or other of them, more or less related to, dependent upon, or to be affected by the result.

"It is believed that a COURT OF ARBITRATION will obviate these difficulties," and, if uniting the principles of law and equity with the established and notorious usages of trade and commerce, general and local, as its standard of right and rule of judgment, and adopting "the prompt methods of business men" in the despatch of its work, will "secure speedy and just decisions at a trifling cost in the cases submitted" to its adjudication.

"Institutions of this kind have been established in Europe, and have proved very successful in confining litigation within narrower and cheaper limits. In each of the cities of New York and Philadelphia, a COURT OF ARBITRATION has been successfully established. It has tried, in each city, cases of great importance, and the decisions, it is understood, have been remarkably satisfactory, whilst the time of suitors is much economized and the expense diminished."

Considerations of this kind induced the Board of Trade, years since, to provide, from among its Directors, a "Committee of Arbitration" for the "decision of disputed accounts and contracts and all controversies of a mercantile character brought before them by the members." The experience of the Board, and the example of successful experiment elsewhere, have induced an application by the Board to the General Assembly of the State at its recent session for an amendment of the Charter, authorizing a more complete and satisfactory arrangement for the accomplishment of the same purpose within a larger circle of subjects, and for giving a more effective operation to the final award.

Under the authority of this amendment, the Board of Trade has organized its "Court of Arbitration," and has secured the services, as Judge of the Court, of the HON. JOHN A. INGLIS, whose varied experience in the administration of justice in the courts of law and equity, gives all needed guaranty for the successful and satisfactory result here of the experiment.

For further explanation of the organization and of the modes of instituting and conducting a proceeding therein, and giving effect to the award, reference is made to the Act of Assembly amending the Charter, to the Rules of Court, and the forms of submission which follow.

The Court is now open to those who require its services. Application may be made to the Clerk, MR. GEORGE U. PORTER, where blank forms will be furnished and other information given.

DECATUR H. MILLER,
President Baltimore Board of Trade.

BY-LAWS OF THE BALTIMORE CORN AND FLOUR EXCHANGE, January, 1856

The merchants involved in the purchase and sale of corn and flour found it necessary and convenient for the benefit of their business to form the Corn and Flour Exchange. Their original formation in 1856 was found to be so valuable that by 1860 the organization expanded its membership to include other businessmen as may be seen in the Amendment to its Charter of January, 1860.

Source: Act of Incorporation and By-Laws as Amended of the Baltimore Corn and Flour Exchange Adopted at a Meeting of the Board of Directors held in January, 1856. (Baltimore, 1860.)

 1. We the undersigned, Nathan Tyson, T.R. Matthews, Solomon Corner, Samuel Fenby, T. Whitridge, William Crichton, B.F. Newcomer, I.M. Parr, T.W. Levering, C.D. Hinks, Charles A. Gambrill, William Chestnut, Samuel Hazlehurst, J.B. Brinkley and John S. Williams, desiring to form a Company for agricultural purposes pursuant to the act of the Legislature of Maryland, entitled "An Act to provide for the formation of Corporations for moral, scientific, literary, dramatic, agricultural or charitable purposes, and for the incorporation of uniform volunteer companies, fire engines, or hose companies, and benevolent, beneficial and musical associations," passed May 13, 1852, chapter 231, to be called "The Baltimore Corn and Flour Exchange," and they and all other subscribers or persons who may hereafter be holders of the stock hereinafter mentioned by the name of "The Baltimore Corn and Flour Exchange," for agricultural purposes aforesaid, their object and intention being to establish a depot or mart for the sale and purchase of grain, flour, provisions, and produce generally where all persons who are subscribers or stockholders as hereinafter mentioned, desiring, can sell or purchase the same. And also to have a Reading Room attached, where there shall be constantly kept a regular list of the Price Currents of said produce from all the important markets, and that the said corporation shall have perpetual succession, with power to sue and be sued, to make and use a common seal, and alter the same at pleasure.

 2. The said Corporation shall have power in and by their corporate name to purchase, lease, hold, convey and mortgage real or leasehold estate in the city of Baltimore, and to erect thereon a building suitable for the purposes as may in the opinion of a majority of the subscribers or stockholders of said Corporation, tend to carry out the design of such institution

and promote the convenient transaction of the business between Farmers and dealers in grain, flour and provisions in the city of Baltimore; and when said building shall have been leased or erected, they shall have power to lease or sub-lease the same, and receive the rents and profits thereof, and divide the same among the stockholders.

3. The capital stock of said Corporation shall consist of not less than one thousand dollars, with liberty to increase the same when a majority of the stockholders or subscribers shall so determine, to any amount not exceeding fifty thousand dollars. The said capital shall be divided into shares of ten dollars each, and the same shall be deemed personal property, and shall be transferable in such manner as the by-laws of such Corporation may direct. The said Corporation may commence business and shall be deemed fully organized when one thousand dollars shall have been fully subscribed and paid in.

4. All the affairs, concerns and business of such Corporation shall be managed and conducted by and under the direction of fifteen directors, who shall be stockholders or subscribers and citizens of Baltimore -- of the State of Maryland, --and who shall be elected by the stockholders or subscribers annually, on the first Monday of January in each year, by ballot, by plurality of the votes of the subscribers or stockholders present or represented by proxy, each share having one vote; and if for any cause such election shall not be then so held, the said Corporation shall not be deemed dissolved, but such election shall be held within six months thereafter. Notice of the time and place of every such election shall be published for one week preceding the day appointed therefor, in two of the daily newspapers printed and published in the city of Baltimore. . . .

9. All persons or firms, residents of the city of Baltimore, of State of Maryland, who subscribe and pay in advance ten dollars, and contract to pay ten dollars in advance thereafter annually, shall be considered as owning one share of stock in said company whilst so subscribing and paying in advance -- to be forfeited to the Corporation when he or they cease to pay the same annually in advance: Provided, that nothing herein contained shall prevent the directors from fixing, in their discretion, the annual payment in advance, at a sum not less than five dollars not more than twenty dollars to each individual or firm subscribing, thereby constituting them stockholders or subscribers.

The funds of the Corporation hereby created shall be alone responsible for the debts and contracts of the Corporation hereby created.

This Act of Incorporation shall take effect immediately from and after the recording of the same in the Clerk's office of the Superior Court of Baltimore city, pursuant to law, and continue in force until the first day of March, 1890. . . .

AMENDMENT

To the Charter of The Baltimore Corn and Flour Exchange, Incorporated under Articles of Association entered into on the twenty-second day of May, 1855, and duly recorded in the office of the Clerk of the Superior Court for Baltimore City.

Now Therefore, we the . . . Directors of the Baltimore Corn and Flour Exchange, do hereby declare and make known that the name and title of The Baltimore Corn and Flour Exchange, aforesaid, has been changed to that of The Corn and Flour Exchange of the city of Baltimore, and by said last mentioned name shall hereafter be known for the purposes contemplated in the aforesaid Original Charter, and we do further make known that Article IV of the Charter, aforesaid, has been amended, so as to read as follows:

4th. All the affairs, concerns and business of such Corporation shall be managed and conducted by and under the direction of fifteen Directors, who shall be stockholders or subscribers, and shall be transacting business in the city of Baltimore, and who shall be known to have a place of business in the city of Baltimore, and who shall be citizens of the State of Maryland, and who shall be elected by the stockholders or subscribers, annually, on the first Monday of January in each year, by ballot, by plurality of the votes of the subscribers or stockholders present, each share having one vote; and if for any cause such election shall not be then so held, the said Corporation shall not be deemed dissolved, but such election shall be held within six months thereafter. Notice of the time and place of every such election shall be published for one week preceding the day appointed therefor, in two of the daily newspapers printed and published in the city of Baltimore.

And we do further make known that Article IX of the Charter aforesaid, has been amended so as to read as follows: 9th. All persons or firms transacting business in the city of Baltimore, and who shall be known to have a place of business in the city of Baltimore, who subscribe and pay in advance ten dollars, and contract to pay ten dollars in advance thereafter annually, shall be considered as owning one share of stock in said Company whilst so subscribing and paying in advance -- to be forfeited to the Corporation when he or they cease to pay the same annually in advance: Provided, that nothing herein contained shall prevent the Directors from fixing, in their discretion, the annual payment in advance, at a sum not less than five dollars nor more than twenty dollars to each individual or firm subscribing, thereby constituting them stockholders or subscribers. . .

ESTABLISHMENT OF THE PEABODY INSTITUTE, 1857

George Peabody, financier and public benefactor, was interested in presenting the City of Baltimore with an institute which would aid in improving the moral and intellectual tone of its citizens. This plan included a Research Library, public lectures, an Academy of Music, a Gallery of Art, and headquarters for the Maryland Historical Society. In addition, prizes were to be awarded to the top high school graduates in the city. The Maryland Legislature issued a charter for the Institute on March 9, 1858, and the Peabody Institute was dedicated, October 25, 1866

Source: Peabody Institute, Baltimore. The Founder's Letters, and the Papers Relating to Its Dedication and its History up to the First January, 1868. (Baltimore, 1868.)

Baltimore, February 12, 1857

Gentlemen:

In pursuance of a purpose long entertained by me, and which I communicated to some of you more than two years ago, I have determined, without further delay, to establish and endow an institute in this City, which, I hope, may become useful towards the improvement of the moral and intellectual culture of the inhabitants of Baltimore, and collaterally to those of the State; and also, towards the enlargement and diffusion of a taste for the Fine Arts.

My wishes in regard to the scope and character of this Institute are known to some of you through a personal communication of my purpose. . . .

In presenting to you the object I propose, I wish you to understand that the details proper to its organization and government and its future control and conduct, I submit entirely to your judgment and discretion; and the perpetuity of that control I confide to you and your successors, to be appointed in the manner prescribed in this letter.

You and your successors will constitute a Board of Trustees, twenty-five in number, to be maintained in perpetual succession, for the accomplishment, preservation and supervision of the purposes for which the Institute is to be established. To you and your successors, therefore, I hereby give full and exclusive power to do whatsoever you may deem most advisable, for the foundation, organization and management of the proposed Institute: and to that end I give to you, and will place at your disposal to be paid to you as you may require, for the present, $300,000, to be expended by you in such manner as you may determine to be most conducive to the effective and early establishment and future maintenance and support of such an Institute as you may deem best adapted to fulfill my intentions as expressed in this letter.

In the general scheme and organization of the Institute, I wish to provide --

First. -- For an extensive Library to be well furnished in every department of knowledge, and of the most approved literature; which is to be maintained for the free use of all persons who may desire to consult it, and be supplied with every proper convenience for daily reference, and study, within appointed hours of the week days of every year. It should consist of the best works on every subject embraced within the scope of its plan, and as completely adapted, as the means at your command may allow, to satisfy the researches of students who may be engaged in the pursuit of knowledge not ordinarily attainable in the private libraries of the country. . . . I recommend, . . . that it shall not be constructed upon the plan of a circulating library; and that the books shall not be allowed to be taken out of the building, except in very special cases, and in accordance with rules adapted to them as exceptional privileges.

Second -- I desire that ample provision and accomodation be made for the regular periodical delivery at the proper season in each year, of lectures by the most capable and accomplished scholars and men of science, within the power of the Trustees to procure. These lectures should be directed to instructions in science, art and literature. They should be established with such regulations as, in the judgment of the Trustees, shall be most effectual to secure the benefits expected from them; and should, under proper and necessary restrictions adapted to preserve good order and guard against abuse, be open to the resort of respectable inhabitants of both sexes, of the City and State; such prices of admission being required as may serve to defray a portion of the necessary expenses maintaining the lectures without impairing their usefulness to the community.

In connection with this provision, I desire that the Trustees in order to encourage and reward merit, should adopt a regulation by which a number of the graduates of the public High Schools of the City, not exceeding fifty of each sex, in each year, who shall have obtained by their proficiency in their studies and their good behaviour, certificates of merit from the Commissioners or superintending authorities of the Schools to which they may be attached, may, by virtue of such certificates, be entitled, as an honorary mark of distinction, to free admission to the lectures for one term or season after obtaining the certificates.

I also desire that for the same purpose of encouraging merit, the Trustees shall make provision for an annual grant of $1200 of which $500 shall be distributed every year, in money prizes, graduated according to merit, of sums not less than $50 nor more than $100 for each prize, to be given to such graduates of the public Male High Schools now existent or which may hereafter be established, as shall, in each year, upon examination and certificate of the School Commissioners, or other persons having the chief superintendance of the same, be adjudged most worthy, from their fidelity to their studies, their attainments, their moral deportment, their personal habits of cleanliness and propriety or manners: the sum of $200 to be appropriated to the purchase in every year of gold medals of two degrees of which ten shall be of the value of $10 each and 20 of the value of $5 each, to be annually distributed to the most meritorious of the graduating classes of the public Female High Schools; these prizes to be adjudged for the same merit, and under the like regulations, as the prizes to be given to the graduates of the Male High Schools. The remaining $500 to be, in like manner, distributed in money prizes, as provided above for the graduates of the Male High School, in the same amounts respectively, to the yearly graduates in the School of Design attached to the Mechanics Institute of this City. . . .

Third -- I wish also that the Institute shall embrace within its plan an Academy of Music, adapted, in the most effective manner, to diffuse and cultivate a taste for that, the most refining of all arts. By providing a capacious and suitably furnished saloon, the facilities necessary to the best exhibitions of the art, the means of studying its principles and practising its compositions, and periodical concerts, aided by the best talent and most eminent skill within their means to procure, the Trustees may promote the purpose to which I propose to devote this department of the Institute. . . .

Fourth -- I contemplate with great satisfaction, as an auxiliary to the improvement of the taste, and, through it, the moral elevation of the character of the society of Baltimore, the establishment of a Gallery of Art in the department of Painting and Statuary. It is therefore, my wish that such a gallery should be included in the plan of the Institute and that spacious and appropriate provision be made for it. It should be supplied, to such an extent as may be practicable, with the works of the best masters, and be placed under such regulations as shall secure free access to it, during stated periods each year, by all orderly and respectable persons who may take an interest in works of this kind; . . .

Lastly -- I desire that ample and convenient accomodation may be made in the building of the Institute for the use of the Maryland Historical Society, of which I am and have long been a member. It is my wish that the Society should permanently occupy its appropriate rooms as soon as they are provided, and should at the proper time when this can be done, be appointed by the Trustees to be the guardian and protector of the property of the Institute; . . .

I am, with great respect,

Your friend,
GEORGE PEABODY

CORRESPONDENCE IN REGARD TO THE BURNING OF RAILROAD BRIDGES IN BALTIMORE, May 9, 1861

The State of Maryland was a border state with sympathies for both the Northern and Southern causes in the early days of tension which preceded, as well as those which followed the outbreak of the Civil War. There had already been a great deal of agitation on the evening of April 19, when troops from Massachusetts tried to pass through the city. Mayor George Brown and Maryland Governor Hicks reluctantly came to the conclusion that if the United States Government could not be persuaded to prevent the passage of Northern troops through Baltimore that the city would have to take matters into its own hands. The conclusion reached was that the Railroad bridges should be burned. The Governor then refused to admit that he had approved of this measure. The following letters are evidence submitted by Mayor Brown to support his contention that he had not acted unilaterally.

Source: Document G by the Maryland House of Delegates, May 10, 1861. <u>Communication from the Mayor of Baltimore with the Mayor and Board of Police of Baltimore City</u> (Frederick, Maryland, 1861.)

<u>To the Honorable,</u>
<u>The General Assembly of Maryland:</u>

In the report recently made to your honorable body by the Board of Police Commissioners of the city of Baltimore, it is stated that in the great emergency which existed in this city on the 19th ult., it was suggested that the most feasible, if not the only practicable mode, of stopping for a time the approach of troops to Baltimore, was to obstruct the Philadelphia, Wilmington and Baltimore, and the Northern Central Rail Roads, by disabling some of the bridges on both roads. And it is added that -- "his honor, the Mayor, stated to the Board that his Excellency, the Governor, with whom he had a few minutes before been in consultation in the presence of several citizens, concurred in these views."

As this concurrence has since been explicitly denied by his Excellency, Governor Hicks, in an official communication addressed to the Senate of Maryland on the 4th inst., which I have just seen, it is due to myself that

I should lay before you the grounds on which the statement was made to the Board of Police; on which they, as well as myself, acted. I seriously regret that so grave a misunderstanding exists between the Governor and myself on so important a subject.

On the evening of the 19th ult., and after the collision had taken place, I mentioned to Governor Hicks that I had begun to fear it might be necessary to burn the Rial Road bridges, but I did not then, in consequence of intelligence which had been received, think it would be. To which he replied that he had no authority to give such an order.

At about 11 o'clock P.M. of the same day, the Hon. H. Lenox Bond, Geroge W. Dobbin, and John C. Brune, Esqrs., were requested by Governor Hicks and myself, to go to Washington in a special train, which was provided for the purpose, to explain in person the condition of things in Baltimore, and to bear the following communications from Governor Hicks and myself, which were addressed to the President.:

Sir: -- This will be presented to you by the Hon. H. Lenox Bond, George W. Dobbin and John C. Brune Esqrs., who will proceed to Washington by an express train at my request, in order to explain fully the fearful conditions of my affairs in this city. The people are exasperated to the highest degree by the passage of troops, and the citizens are universally decided in the opinion that no more should be ordered to come.

The authorities of the City did their best to-day to protect both strangers and citizens and to prevent a collision, but in vain, and but for their great efforts a fearful slaughter would have occurred.

Under these circumstances, it is my solemn duty to inform you that it is not possible for more soldiers to pass through Baltimore unless they fight their way at every step.

I therefore hope and trust, and most earnestly request, that no more troops be permitted or ordered by the government to pass through the City. If they should attempt it, the responsibility for the bloodshed will not rest upon me.

With great respect your ob't serv't

Geo. W. Brown, Mayor

The following from Governor Hicks was appended to my communication.

To His Excellency
    ABRAHAM LINCOLN
        President of the United States:

I have been in Baltimore City since Tuesday evening last, and cooperated with Mayor G. W. Brown, in his untiring efforts to allay and prevent the excitement and suppress the fearful outbreak as indicated above, and I fully concur in all that is said by him in the above communication.

Very respectfully, your ob't serv't

Thomas H. Hicks
Governor of Maryland
Baltimore, May 9th, 1861.

At about 12 o'clock P.M., the Hon. E. Louis Howe and Marshal George P. Kane called at my house, where Governor Hicks was passing the night, and Marshal Kane informed me that a telegram had been received that other troops were to come to Baltimore over the Northern Central Rail Road. There was also a report that troops were on their way who, it was thought, might even then be at Perryville on their way to Baltimore. Mr. Lowe, Marshal Kane, my brother John Cumming Brown, and myself went immediately to the chamber of Gov. Hicks, and laid the matter before him. The point was pressed that if troops were suddenly to come to Baltimore with a determination to pass through, a terrible collision and bloodshed would take place, and the consequences to Baltimore would be fearful, and that the only way to avert the calamity was to destroy the bridges. To this the Governor replied -- "it seems to be necessary," or words to that effect.

He was then asked by me, whether he gave his consent to the destruction of the bridges, and he distinctly, although apparently with great reluctance, replied in the affirmative. I do not assert that I have given the precise language used by Governor Hicks, but I am very clear that I have stated it with substantial correctness, and that his assent was unequivocal, and in answer to a question by me which elicited a distinct affirmative reply.

After this, but before the interview was over, two gentlemen came into the room, both of them strangers to me, but one was introduced as a brother of Governor Hicks, and I am confident that the assent of the Governor to the burning of the bridges was repeated in the presence of these gentlemen.

I went immediately from the chamber of the Governor to the office of the Marshal of Police, where Charles Howard, Esq., the President of the Board of Police was waiting, and reported to him the assent of the Governor to the destruction of the bridges.

Mr. Howard, or some one else, made a further inquiry as to what had been said by the Governor, whereupon Mr. Lowe, Marshal Kane, and my brother John C. Brown all declared that they were present at the interview, and heard Governor Hicks give his assent.

The order to destroy the bridges was accordingly given, and carried out in the manner already reported to your honorable body.

With great respect your ob't serv't

Geo. W. Brown, Mayor.

CREATION OF ENOCH PRATT FREE LIBRARY, 1882-1886

Enoch Pratt, who had moved to Baltimore, made a substantial fortune in business. He carefully analyzed the needs of his adopted city and came to the conclusion that the establishment of a free circulating library for the use of all citizens of Baltimore would be of invaluable aid in raising the intellectual and moral standards of the city. He presented a building worth $225,000 specifically constructed for the housing of the library as well as the sum of $833,333, 1/3 to the city, the latter sum to be used at the will of the city. In return Baltimore was to perpetually grant $50,000 annually for the upkeep of the library. The city government accepted and prepared the necessary legislation. The Enoch Pratt Free Library was dedicated on January 4, 1886.

Source: The Enoch Pratt Free Library of Baltimore City. <u>Letters and Documents Relating to Its Foundation and Organization with Dedicatory Addresses and Exercises, January 4, 1886</u> (Baltimore, 1886.)

Baltimore, January 21, 1882

To the Honorable the Mayor and City Council of Baltimore

I have for some years contemplated establishing a Free Circulating Library, for the benefit of our whole City, and in pursuance of this plan I have entered into a contract to erect a fireproof building on my Mulberry Street lot, capable of holding 200,000 volumes -- my purpose being to have branches connected with it in the four quarters of the City, under the same management.

The excavation for the foundation has been commenced, and the building will be well advanced this year, and completed in the summer of 1883. It will cost when ready for occupancy about . . . ($225,000), and upon its completion I propose to deed it to the City. The title to all the books and property is to be vested in the City, and I will pay to your Honorable Body, upon its completion, the additional sum of . . . ($833,333 1/3), making . . . ($1,058,333 1/3), provided the City will grant and create an annuity of . . . ($50,000) per annum forever, payable to the Board of Trustees, for the support and maintenance of the Library and its branches.

I propose that a Board of nine Trustees be incorporated for the management of "The Pratt Free Library of the City of Baltimore," the Board to be selected by myself from our best citizens, and all vacancies which shall occur, shall be filled by the Board. The articles of incorporation will contain a provision that no Trustee or officer shall be appointed or removed on religious or political grounds. The Trustees are to receive from the City the quarterly payments and to expend it at their discretion for the purposes of the Library.

It is believed that this annual sum will afford a sufficient fund for the purchase of books, for establishing the branches, and for the general management.

The Trustees will be required to make an annual report to the Mayor and City Council of their proceedings, and of the condition of the Library, and the report will contain a full account of the money received and expended.

This plan is suggested not without due consideration of the power of the City to carry it out. The City is expressly authorized by its charter to accept trusts "for any general corporation purpose, or for the general purposes of education"; and although its power of creating debts is limited by the Constitution of the State, yet as the property of the Library is to belong to the City, and as it will receive a sum of money to be disposed of as it pleases with the engagement only to pay an annual sum for the support of its own Institution, it is believed that such a transaction will not involve the creation of a debt within the meaning of the constitutional prohibition.

I suggest that if the money to be paid by me as above stated, were added to the Sinking Fund, and the Interest carefully funded, it would, in no very long time, pay off the debt of the City; but this is intended only as a suggestion, and the disposal of the money is left to your Honorable Body.

If, however, your Honorable Body should, on mature consideration, be of the opinion that the annual payments proposed would involve the creation of a debt, authority for that may be obtained by complying with the provisions of the Constitution; that is, the debt may be created by the City, provided it be authorized by an act of the General Assembly of Maryland, and by an ordinance of the Mayor and City Council of Baltimore, submitted to the legal voters of the City of Baltimore at such time and place as may be fixed by said ordinance, and approved by a majority of the votes cast at such time and place. I cannot but think that such an authority from the General Assembly and from the Mayor and City Council of Baltimore, and from a majority of the legal voters of the City, would be Cheerfully given. [This was the procedure which was followed.]

The plan proposed for the support and management of the Library is the result of long and careful consideration, and, I am satisfied, is well adapted to promote the great object in view, the free circulation of the books of a large and ever-growing Library among the people of the whole City. I trust that it will receive the approval of your Honorable Body, and of the citizens of Baltimore.

Enoch Pratt

DEDICATION CEREMONIES -- ENOCH PRATT LIBRARY
January 4, 1886
Address of Hon. James Hodges, Mayor

It is known that Mr. Enoch Pratt in 1882 offered to establish an Institution in this community to be known as "The Enoch Pratt Free Library of Baltimore City," upon certain conditions, and that the Mayor and City Council of Baltimore, being authorized and empowered by the Legislature of Maryland to do so, accepted his proposal. . . .

. . . Now, we have assembled to-day to inaugurate, with appropriate ceremonies, the Library thus established, and for which such ample provision has been made. It is a notable event in the history of Baltimore, and marks an epoch in its progress. . . .

We pride ourselves, and not without justice, on our public schools. We have determined that no member of the community, so far as we can prevent it, shall be debarred from his share of the common heritage, and we make the opportunities of education as broad as a generous public-school system could effect it.

But, in doing this, we place the key of knowledge into the student's hand. It is another task to fill the treasury into which that key opens. Thus the public library is the complement of the public school, and carries on the work which that has begun. For education is not an absolute, but a relative good; all depends upon the use that is made of it. . . .

Though I will not say that a zeal for learning has ever eaten up the people of Baltimore, or that we have aspired to the distinction of "the Athens of America," yet we have never wanted those who loved, and who helped forward liberal studies and tastes. The noble library that we open today is the successor of a line of libraries founded or assisted by private liberality. . . .

Truly Baltimore has had reason to be proud of her citizens; of some who are still with us, and of some who have departed; men, who, like Peabody, Hopkins, Moses Sheppard, Thomas Wilson and others, have recognized that they were but stewards of the wealth with which providence had blessed them, and held it in trust for uses of good. Such a citizen is he who has founded this noble Institution, and, as with George Peabody and Johns Hopkins, and Sheppard and Wilson, Baltimore is the City of his adoption, not of his nativity.

I have known that citizen for forty years, and few outside of his daily associates, have had a better opportunity of learning his characteristics. For nearly three years we served together on the Board of Commissioners of Finance of this City, and there I saw exemplified those traits of character which have given Enoch Pratt so eminent a reputation as a merchant and financier. He combines, to an extra-ordinary degree, breadth and penetration of intellectual vision, his comprehension of financial propositions is almost instantaneous, and as prompt and sure is his power to winnow the grain from the chaff, and note an unsound spot in a plausible scheme.

As a merchant, respected for his wisdom, honored for his integrity, he has lived among us for the greater part of a long life. At once energetic and unobtrusive, he has never sought posts of honor, nor ever shirked posts of duty. His hand has been felt for good in public affairs, when few knew the guiding spirit; and his quiet voice has given wise counsel and asked no need of praise.

With him, temperament and judgment are so evenly balanced that his determination is almost intuitive, and rarely needs reconsideration. His confidence is not lightly given, nor, when given, is it lightly shaken. It is a plant of slow growth, but it strikes its roots deep and strong.

Mr. Pratt's fortune was not won by speculation; it is not the unwilling tribute paid by rashness or folly, to shrewdness or craft. It has been the steady accumulation of a life devoted to legitimate business. He saw his purposes clearly before him, as the mariner sees his guiding star, and he never deviated from his course, until his voyage was successfully accomplished. Nor did he seek fortune for the mere sake of accumulation, and to be pointed out as a rich man. . . .

Few have surpassed him in the power of close and minute investigation into details and nothing relative to any plan under his consideration, escapes his observation, or is denied its due weight. In the choice of co-operators, and in the direction of their activity, he has shown that high administrative power which in the fields of commerce and finance, as in other fields, makes the leader of men.

The instruction of the people has always been near to the heart of Mr. Pratt. The foundation of this library is a natural sequence to the Pratt Free School which he founded in 1865 in Middleborough, Massachusetts, which is still in successful operation. From that time to this he has evolved plans for educational advancement.

Desirous of bestowing some worthy gift upon his fellow-citizens of Baltimore, he concluded that one of the greatest needs of the City was a free public library. The Peabody Library is a grand foundation, worthy of the generous man to whom it owes its existence, and its stores are of inestimable value; but it is of a different character, and meets other wants. Mr. Pratt's design was to found a library of good reading for the entire public, of books which might be read at the fireside, and should carry their stores of knowledge, of beauty, or of innocent recreation, to the homes of the people. The plan, as the founder matured it, . . . consists of a central collection, worthily -- indeed magnificently -- housed, with branches in several sections of the city, each branch to be a minor but representative library, and all in communication with the Central Library and its ample stores.

* * *

REPORT OF THE CHARTER COMMISSION,
January 27, 1898

The commission made a careful study of the
needs of the municipal Government and presented a New Charter for the city based on
eight principles which included responsibility
of municipal officials, representation of minority party interests, holding of elections for
city officials at different times than federal and
state elections to eliminate outside political issues from influencing elections, appointment of
experts to departments, limiting of method and
time of granting of use of public property, creating of financial responsibility, removal of the
public school system from political influence,
and regulation of the care of the sick and poor.
This was an important advance for Home Rule
in Baltimore although the city was not able to
regain control of police matters.

Source: Report of the Charter Commission of 1898 in Article 4, Public Laws (City of Baltimore) containing the Charter of Baltimore City, and the Miscellaneous Local Laws, with any Additions Made by the General Assembly of 1927, . . . (Baltimore, 1927.)

Baltimore, January 27, 1898

To the Honorable General Assembly of Maryland:

    The Commission appointed pursuant to the ordinance of the Mayor and City Council of Baltimore, approved November 24, 1897, to draft a new Charter for the City of Baltimore, herewith, as directed by said ordinance, respectfully submit the result of their labors.

    After mature deliberation the Commission decided at the beginning of their work of preparing a new organic Act for the City of Baltimore, to be governed by certain well-defined and recognized principles relating to municipal government, which had been found in other cities to be beneficial and which it was thought were fundamental and necessary, if there were to be an improvement on the present law relating to the City of Baltimore some of these controlling principles were:

    1. To locate responsibility upon public officials in such a manner that it could not be evaded.

    2. To give representation to the minority party in all departments, when composed of more than one person, so that an opportunity might be

given to the minority to scrutinize the actions of the party in power.

3. To hold municipal elections of a different time from the State and Federal elections, in order to separate municipal affairs from the influence of the political issues which are necessarily involved in State and Federal elections.

4. To require the appointment of experts in all departments where professional knowledge and skill are required.

5. To grant the use of the states and other public property for limited terms, and to the highest bidder, subject to the control and regulation of the city during the period of the grant.

6. To check hasty legislation, especially in matters relating to expenditure of the public moneys, and to prohibit the creation of floating debts.

7. To remove the public school system from all possible political influence.

8. To place the indigent sick and poor, when their treatment, care or support is paid for by the city, under the supervision of city officials.

DOCUMENTS

ANNUAL MESSAGE OF MAYOR THOMAS G. HAYES,
September 17, 1900

Mayor Thomas G. Hayes was the first mayor under the New Charter of 1898 approved by the Maryland Legislature. In this Annual Message he praised the attributes of the new charter, indicating how he had already taken action to reorganize the administration of the city under its provisions. In particular he praised the establishment of the Board of Awards which would help to guarantee the impartial granting of contracts by the city under a system which would provide greater economies. He did deplore the fact that the administration of the police Force had been removed from the city government and place in the hands of the state. On the other hand, the establishment of a new school board free from political control would seemingly guarantee the creation of a fine public education system for the city.

Source: Annual Message of Hon. Thomas G. Hayes, Mayor, to the City Council of Baltimore, September 17, 1900 in Baltimore. Reports of the City Officers and Departments, 1899 (Baltimore, 1900.)

Baltimore, September 17, 1900

To the Honorable the Members of the City Council:
Gentlemen:
* * *

Organization of Heads of Departments

On the second of March, 1900, I directed the heads of departments, which have only advisory powers, as prescribed in the New Charter to organize. The Superintendent of Public Buildings fitted up a room in the City Hall for their first and subsequent meetings. On this date, in person, I supervised the organization of the Departments of Finance, Public Safety, Public Improvements, Charities and Corrections, and Reviews and Assessment. I had provided substantially bound volumes for each department and directed that the minutes of each meeting be recorded by the Secretary, who was elected by each department at their first meeting.

These departments have held regular monthly meetings, and such matters as have come before them have been considered and disposed of.

This feature of the New Charter relative to these advisory heads of departments is most admirable, as by the organization of these advisory boards the Mayor is furnished with an advisory body on the different questions relating to their respective departments, such as finance, Public Safety, Public Improvements, Charities and Corrections, and Review and Assessment.

In addition to the advisory powers of these boards, each head of a sub-department, included in a department is required to become familiar with the operation and working of every other sub-department in its department.

I shall never hesitate to bring into operation the advisory powers of these departments whenever the public interests require.

In the organization of both the departments and sub-departments I endeavored to impress upon the members of these departments and sub-departments the fact that the policy of the present administration was to give to the people of Baltimore an honest and economical city administration, and that I should look to these municipal officials to aid me in carrying out this policy. They were informed that under the New Charter they had the sole power in administering their respective departments and sub-departments and that this power brought a responsibility which I should rigidly enforce.

* * *

Board of Awards

One of the most important boards created by the New Charter is the Board of Awards. This board controls absolutely the making of all contracts by the city for work or supplies when the amount is or exceeds $500. The municipal officials who are ex officio members of this board, are the Mayor, Comptroller, City Register, City Solicitor, and President of the Second Branch of the City Council.

The provision of the New Charter relating to the duties and powers of this board ensure fair competition and secure the awarding of all contracts to the lowest responsible bidders after due advertisement. The original draft of all specifications and ads are prepared by the sub-department needing the work or supplies, this board then reviews these specifications and advertisements, and if the former ensure fair competition and are right in all respects, the board approves them and its president signs the same. This requirement of supervising both specifications and advertisements by this board is not a requirement of the New Charter, but solely the action of the board by its own resolution. This supervision by the board of all specifications and advertisements is most proper and has been most beneficial. . . .

I have instructed every department and sub-department, when they make purchases for less than $500 for the use of their respective departments and sub-departments, to follow the same rule, and by advertisement or otherwise to ensure competition and get the articles at the very lowest cash price.

A failure of a department or sub-department to faithfully observe this requirement will be cause for instant removal. I am determined that the city shall receive the benefit of competition in all its purchases. There can be no favoritism shown in the purchase of either supplies or work, whether the amount is above or below $500.00. Every contractor or furnisher of supplies or work can feel assured that if he is the lowest responsible bidder, he will get the contract, and hence may with safety and security bid at his lowest cash price. Any municipal official or employee who dares use the influence of his office to aid a favorite in getting a contract will be instantly dismissed from the municipal service. And if he has taken, or agreed to take, a bribe in commission, or any other consideration, in addition to his dismissal he shall be prosecuted for the crime of bribery, and the city's law department shall aid in his prosecution. I am determined that in the matter of awarding, as well as in executing contracts, absolute honesty shall be observed, and that no commission or rakeoffs, paid by bidders to municipal officials or employees shall be tolerated during my administration of the city government.

In addition to the great moral turpitude and criminality of such conduct, if the bidder can offer to pay a municipal official or employee a commission for his aid or assistance in getting a city contract, he must in his bid give the amount of the commission to the taxpayers and not to the corrupt municipal offical or employee.

Police Board

The existing law inflicts a great wrong on the people of Baltimore in refusing to give them any direct representation on the Police Board. The making of this board, exclusively a State organization, and refusing to the municipality any voice in the organization or management of this board, is not only violative of the principle of home rule, so essential to good local government, but compels the taxpayers to contribute annually nearly $1,000,000 for the support of this service, and at the same time makes nobody immediately responsible to them for the accountability of this large expenditure. Impressed with the wrong of this law, in my official capacity, I appeared before the last Legislature and asked that the General Assembly give to the people of Baltimore a representative on this board, but to my appeal a deaf ear was turned. The police force, like the public schools, should be taken and kept out of the touch or influence of partisan politics, but the making of the Mayor of Baltimore, the president, or a member of this board, in no way introduces politics into the management of this force. . . .

* * *

Department of Finance
* * *

Much of the benefit which has accrued to the municipal government of Baltimore is attributable to the wise provisions of the New Charter. Especially is this true as to the finances of the city. When the New Charter went into effect the finances of this city were in a wretched condition. An enormous funded debt existed, and a tax rate which was not only oppressive but rendered real estate, which paid the most of these taxes, in the opinion of some unmarketable. It is this improved financial system imposed by the New Charter of our city to which I desire to refer.

As a member of the Charter Commission which drafted this new organic Act, I am familiar with the discussions relating to a change in our financial system, which occurred during the meetings of that body. My own position, as a member of that commission, in these discussions, was well known. I early maintained that the then financial system of Baltimore was radically wrong, and should be absolutely abandoned. The point of my contention was the the city government was run on credit or temporary loan basis, while it should be conducted on a strictly cash basis, or pay as you go.

Some thought this could not be done. I insisted that in the management of the financial affairs of a municipal corporation the cash basis was as available as with a private corporation.

I was entrusted by my colleagues of the commission with the putting of the views as to the financial system for the city, expressed to them, into the draft of a law.

This I had the honor to do, and it is now a part of the New Charter. It must be remembered that the financial system of the city before the New Charter was to borrow money whenever needed by a temporary loan; this temporary loan became a floating debt, and when the floating debts became too large to carry as such, they were funded, and a bonded indebtedness created, and the people then for the first time were informed of this silent growing floating debt, that is, when it was funded, and they were taxed for a sinking fund to pay the bonds.

This, in my opinion, was the very worst kind of financiering. It not only kept the people in ignorance of the spending of the moneys obtained by temporary loans and floating debts, but it gave rise to great extravagance, and a large increase of the bonded indebtedness of the city. The provision at the threshold of this new financial system was to prohibit by law and make null and void in the future any temporary loan or floating debt, with the single exception of allowing a temporary loan to be met by taxes then in process of collection. Again the inviolability of the sinking fund was emphatically declared. This fund, which in the past had been robbed and its moneys diverted to uses not only illegal but in the teeth of the provisions of ordinances creating the fund, was sacredly guarded, and by provisions of the new system its funds were increased, so as to make up the deficiencies which had occurred by reason of the wrongful diversion of its monies to uses foreign to its purpose. . . .

Another provision of the Charter's financial system was the fixing of the minimum tax rate by an administrative board, the Board of Estimates, that is to say, this board were to ascertain what rate of taxation was necessary to meet the annual expenses, and the City Council in making the levy could not lessen this rate as so fixed. This prevented the occurance of an annual deficiency to be taken care of at the close of each year.

When this system was presented, the author had no precedent to guide him or test of its success as a system, but he thought in theory and principle it was right and would be beneficial. . . .

* * *

Department of Education

The changes made in this department by the New Charter are most beneficial to the interests of public education.

It is unfortunate that in most large cities, Baltimore not excepted, partisan politics has had a most material and injurious influence and effect in the management of public education. Nothing should be more appreciated by the people of this city than the provisions of their New Charter which absolutely removes our public schools from the touch or influence, either directly or indirectly of politics. In the appointment of teachers under this law merit and fitness are the sole requirements for appointment, and no human influence or pull can possibly be invoked to effect the appointment.

The New Charter puts our public schools, so far as appointment of teachers is concerned, under the most rigid rules of the civil service. This is exactly as it should be. The term of teachers is now for life, efficiency and good behavior.

I was fortunate in prevailing upon some of our best citizens to accept the positions of school commissioners, and they have faithfully performed the duties of their offices.

The Board of Schools Commissioners, by the Charter, are given a degree of independence not possessed by any other board in the municipal government. The City Council only votes the money needed for the maintenance of the schools, and this ends its power or control over this board.

The Commissioners (not the Board of Awards) advertise and make their own contracts for text books, stationery and furniture. All plans for school building emanate from the school commissioners.

This power conferred on this board was intended to give them absolute independence of outside influence and control, and fix the responsibility for the conduct of the schools on the members of the board. If we do not have the very best public school system to be had, the fault is solely with the Board of School Commissioners, or the Mayor, who permits to exist an inefficient board. I consider our public schools to be the great bulwark of our civil liberty, and their efficiency should be maintained at all hazards.

* * *

Respectfully submitted.

Thomas G. Hayes, Mayor

ORDINANCE REGULATING PERFORMANCE OF
"THE STAR SPANGLED BANNER,"
July 7, 1916

Much controversy arose over the playing of "The Star Spangled Banner" because it was not performed separately from other musical pieces. Consequently, the city of Baltimore felt that since it was the location where the National Anthem had been composed, it should determine the conditions under which it could be rendered.

Source: Ordinance No. 167. <u>Ordinances and Resolutions of the Mayor and City Council of Baltimore. Passed at the Annual Session 1916-17</u> (Baltimore, 1917), pp. 47-49.

No. 167

An Ordinance regulating the manner and places in which "The Star Spangled Banner" may be played, sung or rendered.

WHEREAS, "The Star Spangled Banner" is universally recognized as the National Anthem of our country and has been adopted as such by both the War and Navy Departments of our Government, and by reason of the fact that the City of Baltimore was the place of its composition, it is fitting that Baltimore should take suitable action to maintain its character as the National Anthem; and

WHEREAS, the indiscriminate rendition of "The Star Spangled Banner," or parts thereof in connection with other compensations tends to lower the esteem and reverence in which the National Anthem should be held by the people of our Nation, and to prevent its desecration;

Now Therefore --

Section 1. Be it ordained by the Mayor and City Council of Baltimore, that "The Star Spangled Banner" shall not be played, sung or rendered in the City of Baltimore in any public place, or at any public entertainment, or in any theatre or moving picture hall, restaurant or cafe, except as an entire and separate composition or number, without embellishments of national or other melodies, nor shall "The Star Spangled Banner" be played at or in any of the places mentioned for dancing or as an exit march; and whenever and wherever practicable, the musicians, performers or other persons shall stand while playing, singing or rendering "The Star Spangled Banner." Any person violating the provisions of this Section shall be guilty of a misdemeanor, and upon conviction thereof before a Court of competent jurisdiction of this State shall be fined not more than $100.

Section 2. And be it further ordained, no owner, proprietor or manager of any theatre, moving picture hall, or restaurant, cafe or other place in the City of Baltimore where the public gathers shall permit or allow anyone playing, singing or performing therein to play, sing or render "The Star Spangled Banner" in violation of the provisions of the aforegoing section, and in the event of any such permission or allowance such owner, proprietor or manager upon conviction thereof shall be subject to the penalties imposed by the foregoing Section.

Section 3. And be it further ordained, the City Librarian is hereby authorized and directed to have copies of this ordinance printed and distributed to all the theatres, moving picture halls, restaurants and cafes and to the offices of all musical unions or branches thereof in the City of Baltimore at least ten days before this ordinance shall go into effect, the expenses thereof to be paid out of the funds of the City Librarian not otherwise appropriated.

Section 4. And be it further ordained, that this ordinance shall take effect from the date of its passage.

Approved July 7, 1916.

James H. Preston, Mayor.

BALTIMORE LAND AND TRANSPORTATION PROPOSALS, 1919

This report presented by the Planning Commission presented general concepts of urban development and specific plans which would leave vacant land for municipal buildings, including schools, and parks. In addition the committee recognized the need for concerted action with the railroads to develop the harbor facilities in order to retain Baltimore's commercial prominence.

Source: Report of the City Planning Committee of the City of Baltimore, Maryland. "Development of the Territory Added under the Act of 1918, Together with Recommendations and Suggestions on the Railroad, Rapid Transit, and Harbor Problems of the City." (Baltimore, May 1, 1919.)

* * *
Street Plans
* * *

It is recommended that at the time any main avenues are definitely laid down, sufficient property be acquired by the municipality at their principle converging points so as to provide sites for such public buildings as schools, fire houses, or police stations. In this matter the strategic value of such points would be utilized to the full, to increase the efficiency of those municipal activities whose accessibility to all points within a given area are to be desired. Upon the plan many such points have been indicated. . . .

Harbor Development
* * *

Geography offers Baltimore the opportunity of becoming one of the centers of world commerce. All the Atlantic coast rail traffic between the north and south passes through it; it is the natural outlet for the Middle West. The development of the Chesapeake and Delaware Canal under government ownership will bring passed the mouth of the Patapsco River a great volume of freight which now passes outside the capes. It now is a harbor practically free from ice an average tide of only fourteen inches, a thirty-five foot channel to the sea, and a freight differential in its favor established by the government. It has ample dry-dock facilities. . . .

* * *

No real solution can be hoped for until the whole waterfront can be treated as a single unit. Many cities are striving for this by the adoption of a policy of an extension of municipally owned docks, with the end in view of ultimately acquiring all such property. Should the railroad entering Baltimore reach with the city some form of agreement as to unit terminal operation, they, together with the city, would control a great portion of the present harbor development.

BALTIMORE PLAN FOR POSTWAR ACTIVITY, 1943

The city government was determined to avoid the difficulties that had been encountered at the end of the First World War by presenting plans well in advance of the establishment of peace after the Second World War. As a result, Mayor Howard Jackson appointed a committee to present proposals. One of the suggestions was taken up by many industries throughout the nation: deferred maintenance. Under this plan the government would permit industries to invest funds which they would normally use for replacement and repair of equipment in special bonds. This money would be returned to the companies in semi-annual installments over a period of three or four years, tax-free, as long as the money was then used for repair and replacement.

Source: Baltimore Committee for Post-War Planning. Baltimore Plan for Postwar Activity by Citizens to Restore Business, Preserve Private Enterprise, Promote Useful Public Works, and Increase Employment. A Progress Report to Mayor Howard W. Jackson by the Citizens' Committee (Baltimore, 1943.)

Reasons for a Baltimore post-war Committee

Your Committee was appointed with the aim of guiding Baltimore through the difficulties of a post-war period. This includes both the plans to avoid any dangers of that period and to put our city in the most advantageous position possible. We should try to avoid the dangers of large unemployment, dangers which may be particularly grave for us, not only because of an enormous influx of war workers, but also because of the effects now in sight upon the peace time employment in industries and commercial concerns resulting from the classification of Baltimore as a critical area. This diverts to other centers the goods and services these industries normally provide in order to release workers to war activities. It also results in contraction in employment forces of such concerns through the departure of employees for the armed forces and war industry employment. The real problem is how many of these establishments can survive these processes through the war period and be available as post-war sources of employment. These businesses include some highly important ones that have for generations in periods of prosperity and depression been a permanent and stabilizing section of the industrial backbone of our City. They have heretofore provided goods essential to both civilian and war needs, but are being excluded from war orders to ease the local labor shortage in war industries. . . .

Our Port

Baltimore has benefitted from the fact that it is the "farthest west of the eastern ports" and it has become the center of a vast network of railroads and highways. However, the interest of its people, and the helpful efforts in the past of the Baltimore Association of Commerce and other agencies, must be continued. If Baltimore is to take its proper place in the promotion of the greater world commerce which will accompany a successful peace, and particularly the expected growth in Latin American Trade, the port itself and the rail and highway terminals serving it must be carefully studied and completely planned. . . .

II. Reserves

Savings in capital expenditures by the State of Maryland and the City of Baltimore should be set aside in special reserve funds to provide against possible increase in unemployment and the need for public facilities which can't be expanded normally under existing conditions. Such reserve will serve to provide work for those returning from the armed forces and war industries, provide needed enlargement of public projects and obviate the necessity for imposing additional taxes on a citizenry which will then be bearing a tax burden so large as to constitute a definite menace to a return to normal living and operating conditions. . . .

"Deferred Maintenance"; What Is It?

Deferred Maintenance can be described very simply. As one example; there still exist, as museum pieces, some of the first railroad locomotives. They have been well housed, cleaned and painted and their maintenance is good, but as far as any practical use is concerned they are 100% depreciated through obsolescence. On the other hand, a locomotive may be of the most modern type and because of difficulties in obtaining supplies and skilled labor may be in very bad condition. It is in no way depreciated but its maintenance has been deferred.

For another example, an industry or business may spend in normal times a million dollars a year for labor and material to keep its plant and equipment in good operating condition. Under war conditions it may have had to reduce this expenditure to $400,000 because it cannot get the material or labor. At the end of the war it will find itself with a run down plant, which in a short time would have to be shut down, or even be abandoned, because of deferred maintenance. If, however, it has been able to put aside each year the $600,000 which it could not spend, it can accomplish three important things for the post-war period:
   1. It can immediately order the material it needs for maintenance, which will provide employment in the material manufacturing plants.
   2. It can hire maintenance men to use this material and restore its plant and equipment to good condition.

3. Through this restoration it can continue to operate and provide jobs and be prepared to expand if necessary.

However, for all business, and particularly for small business, to have such funds available in cash (and they must be in cash), a means of setting aside this money without the penalty of taxation is essential. Money properly spent for necessary maintenance is not taxable. Money put aside for necessary maintenance because it cannot be spent for that purpose but must be readily available immediately after the war, should be similarly non-taxable. This can only be accomplished on a sound scale through a special Treasury bond, payable by the Government at the end of the war over a period of three or four years, probably in installments every six months, with provision that if these funds were not used for deferred maintenance but were distributed, they would then be subject to the taxes.

The Treasury should make available at once such a deferred maintenance bond. Reserves of this kind, if set up by business and by local governments in sufficient amount will accomplish three very important objects.

1. They would bring in large amounts of money to the Federal Government at a time when the Government needs every dollar that can be spared.
2. They would encourage the deferment of all but the most necessary maintenance because it would be known that the maintenance could be made good later.
3. The setting up of proper deferred maintenance in the statements of corporations would give a truer picture of their real earnings to all interested in them.

A large amount of money spent under the careful supervision of private initiative at the close of the war would go far towards obviating a post-war depression.

We are recommending not that the Treasury merely allow this to be done but that the Treasury encourage its being done as a far-sighted policy for the good of the whole country.

ARTERIAL PROPOSAL FOR BALTIMORE, October 9, 1944

Baltimore's traffic had increased since the 1930s. The city government wanted to prepare in advance for the problems which it would face in the postwar years. Robert Moses and other consultants were called in to study the city's traffic pattern and to present proposals for its improvement. The final conclusion was to develop a toll-free expressway through the center of town which would take a great deal of traffic off the main streets.

Source: Robert Moses, Director. *Baltimore Arterial Report* (Baltimore, October 9, 1944.)

October 9, 1944

The Mayor and City Council Baltimore, Maryland

Dear Sirs:

The conclusions summarized in this statement are those of the consultants as detailed reports follow as well as mine. There are nowhere differences of opinion or even mental reservations among us. . . .

First a few general observations:

This is not an academic treatise on planning nor an ideal program made without reference to the local laws, customs, finances and other practical considerations involving public opinion in an old and somewhat conservative community. It would be futile for example for us to have recommended drastic and revolutionary programs which we know would not receive serious consideration by the voters. Similarly, it would be senseless for us to develop any program which would impair the debt or tax structure of the city, or go beyond its resources or would even appear to preempt all funds which may be made available for improvements. On the other hand, it would be shortsighted for the City of Baltimore to fail to take full advantage of all federal and state funds allocated to arterial construction in cities, or by refusing to supplement them to be forced in the end to adopt an inferior plan which would produce no general benefits, . . .

. . . Baltimore might have called in some of our more glittering theoretical planners, in which case this city would have been told how urbanism must be discarded and urged not to waste money on central arteries when the higher strategy calls for the abandonment of most of the town. Instead you have asked for practical advice, no doubt on the shrewd assumption that those who have made plenty of mistakes elsewhere may be valuable in seeing that they are not repeated in Baltimore. . . .

... Urban centers will be made more accessible, not abandoned, and cars, trucks and buses will no longer be left helplessly mired on their outskirts. ...

... We have adopted as a conservative estimate an increase of 35 percent in the number of cars in the Baltimore area between 1938 and 1950. All the indications are that the increase will be even greater. ... Congestion is already serious and will be even worse. ...

We are united in the conclusion that the arterial problem of Baltimore can in a large measure be solved by building an expressway, which we shall call the Franklin Expressway, through the heart of the city, ...

We recommend a genuine municipal improvement of wide scope with depressed express lanes, attractively designed bridges, landscaped slopes, wide service roads and incidental walks and promenades, park and recreational facilities such as are existent in New York and other places have proven successful and popular, and with the planning, financing, construction, and operation of which all of the consultants and I have been identified. If such an improvement is made we have assumed that the people of Baltimore will be willing to protect it against large and obtrusive signs and billboards, ...

We carefully canvassed the possibility of charging tolls on the expressway and came to the conclusion that it is impracticable, primarily because only part of the necessary funds could be raised by the sale of revenue bonds or city bonds secured by toll revenues, and because no time would be gained in construction. ... Finally, we became convinced that more cars, trucks and other vehicles would take advantage of the central express lanes as distinguished from the service roads if there were no tolls, and that therefore an entirely free expressway would go very much farther toward solving the traffic congestion problem. ...

We have not stressed employment, in Baltimore and elsewhere, which would be brought about by the adoption of this plan. This program will be helpful in stimulating recovery. ...

Some 19,000 people live in the path of the Franklin Expressway and will be displaced by it. A good many of them live in what may fairly be characterized as substandard areas. Others occupy reasonably good quarters. The question will arise as to what will become of these people. Many can be housed in temporary war housing projects as war orders are terminated and vacancies occur, and later provide a form of permanent housing in additional postwar federal housing projects, ...

INDUSTRIAL PLANNING IN BALTIMORE, November, 1961

The nature of manufacturing had undergone a change in the post-World War II period. The Department of Planning discussed the changes that had taken place and made recommendations for attracting more industry to the city as well as adding additional land for that purpose.

Source: Department of Planning. Planning for Industry in Baltimore City (Baltimore, 1961.)

KEY CHARACTERISTICS OF MANUFACTURING

Baltimore is generally regarded as an industrial city and employment figures support this belief. Almost one-third of all City workers were employed by manufacturing industries in 1959, and over half were employed by manufacturing and nonmanufacturing industries combined. By comparison retail trade accounted for only about 20 percent of total employment. While industrial employment remains strong, there has been some shift to Services employment in recent years. Between 1948 and 1959 total employment in the City increased slightly, but the partition employed by industry decreased. Manufacturing industry declined from 38 percent to 31 percent, in contrast with the Services group, which increased from 9 percent to 15 percent. Similar shifts occurred in other East Coast industrial centers. . . .

In 1958 Baltimore ranked high among comparable industrial cities in value added by manufacturing per manufacturing employee and metropolitan area figures for the same period show a similar relationship. . . .

Baltimore City (and its metropolitan area) was low in 1950 in the proportion of female employment in the manufacturing force. . . . Female labor was most highly used in Baltimore by the Apparel group, whose employees were 68 percent female at that time. The Textiles industry was also a heavy employer of females -- 53 percent of the workers. . . .

CHARACTERISTICS OF MANUFACTURING FIRMS

A high proportion of Baltimore-City's manufacturing firms are small. 43 percent had less than twenty employees in 1958 as compared with 30 percent in New York City. On the other hand, because of the large number employed by a few firms, the average number of employees per manufacturing establishment is high. In Baltimore City in 1958 there was an average of 69 employees per establishment as compared with 58 in Philadelphia, ...

Only 3 percent of Baltimore City firms employed 500 or more employees, but this small percentage employed 42 percent of the manufacturing labor force. Primary metals and Transportation Equipment are dominant large-firm manufacturing groups; the Printing and Publishing and Non-Electrical Machinery groups are important among small firms. . . .

MANUFACTURING FIRM CHANGES

Manufacturing activities in Baltimore City have undergone considerable change since World War II through creation and abandonment of firms, firm moves to points beyond City limits, and relocation of firms within the City. During the 1948-1958 period, 279 new manufacturing firms were created in the city providing approximately 10,000 new jobs; but 320 firms were abandoned during the same period eliminating about 19,000 jobs. The result was a net loss of 41 firms and approximately 9,000 jobs through creation and abandonment. Manufacturing groups which were particularly heavy losers both in firms and in number of employees, were Apparel and Other Finished Fabric Products and Food and Kindred Products. The Paper and Allied Products and Transportation Equipment groups evidenced the most pronounced gains. . . .

During the 1948-1958 period, 50 established Baltimore manufacturing firms moved to locations outside the City, taking with them almost 5,000 jobs. The Food and Kindred Products, Fabricated Metal Products and Transportation Equipment groups were prominent among these moves. However, there was much more moving within the City than out of it during that period measured both by number of firms and by number of employees involved. There were 346 firm moves within the City. Approximately 75 percent of all such moves had destinations in the five inner sectors of the City, and about half had both origin and destination in the same sector. . . .

VACANT INDUSTRIAL LAND INVENTORY

In June 1961, a field survey indicated that there are in Baltimore approximately 2,150 net acres of vacant land in parcels of one acre or more considered potential for future industrial development. . . .

Completion of two urban renewal projects now in progress will provide an additional 50 net acres of land for future industrial development. . . . The limited amount of vacant land remaining for industrial development in the City suggests the possible need for additional urban renewal projects of this type and other measures such as reclamation of marsh areas.

BALTIMORE CITY CHARTER, 1964

The city charter of Baltimore as revised in 1964 reinforced the issue of home rule for the city. Financial responsibility and accountability were retained and enforced. Uniformity of taxation was maintained.

Source: Charter of Baltimore City: 1964 Revision, As Amended to January, 1969 (Baltimore, 1969.)

BALTIMORE CITY CHARTER

RESOLUTION NO. 1

Resolution amending the Charter of Baltimore City and providing for the submission thereof to the voters of said City for adoption or rejection.

Be it resolved by the Mayor and City Council of Baltimore, That the Charter of Baltimore City, 1949 Ed., as subsequently amended, be amended to read as follows:

ARTICLE I

GENERAL PROVISIONS

1. CORPORATE ENTITY. The inhabitants of the City of Baltimore are a corporation, but the name of the "Mayor and City Council of Baltimore," and by that name shall have perpetual succession, may sue and be sued, may purchase and hold real, personal and mixed property and dispose of the same for the benefit of said City, as herein provided, and may have and use a common seal, which may be altered at pleasure.

2. DEFINITIONS. As used in this Charter, unless the context otherwise requires:

(a) "City" means the Mayor and City Council of Baltimore, the body corporate as established by Section 1 of this Article I.

(b) "Voter" means any person whose name appears on the election records kept by the Board of Supervisors of Elections of Baltimore City, as a qualified voter in said City.

(c) "Charter" means this Charter, composed of Articles I to IX, inclusive, and any amendments and additions thereto which may hereafter be duly adopted; reference herein to Articles and Sections by number are references to Articles and Sections of the Charter.

(d) "Person" means any individual, form, copartnership, corporation, company, association, or body politic except the City; and includes any personal representative, agent, trustee, receiver, assignee or other similar representative thereof.

(e) Except where such construction would be unreasonable, the singular always includes the plural, and vice versa, and the masculine includes all genders.

(f) "Officer" and "municipal officer" shall include, but shall not be limited to, the heads of all departments and bureaus, the members of all commissions and boards, and persons who exercise authority comparable to that of heads of departments or bureaus.

(g) "Term of office" means the period of time for which any person shall have been elected or appointed to hold office, and in addition such time as shall elapse after the expiration of his term until his successor shall have been elected or appointed and qualified.

(h) "Ordinance of Estimates" and "annual Ordinance of Estimates" shall include supplementary appropriation ordinances.

(i) "Subject to the authority" shall mean that the person or body possessed of such authority may amend or revoke the action or decision subject to such authority or reserve to himself or itself such action or decision.

(j) "Municipal agency" shall include all departments, bureaus, boards and commissions and persons not embraced in a department who exercise authority comparable to that of heads of departments or bureaus.

(k) "Street", unless the contrary clearly appears from the context, shall include any public street, boulevard, road, alley, lane, sidewalk, foot-way or other public way owned by the City or habitually used as such by the public.

(l) Whereever provision is made in the Charter that the City Council shall act by a majority or other proportion of its members, the term "members" in the phrase "of its members" shall mean the total number of members provided for by law, including the President, whether or not any vacancies due to death, resignation, disqualification or other cause may then exist. . . .

3. PROPERTY RIGHTS; TRUSTS. All the property and franchises of every kind belonging to, in the possession of, or hereafter acquired by the City are vested in it and it may dispose of any property belonging to it in the manner and upon the terms provided in the Charter. The City may receive in trust, and may control for the purposes of such trust, all moneys and assets which may have been or shall be bestowed upon it by will, deed or any other form of gift or conveyance in trust for any corporate purpose, or in aid of the indigent poor, or for the general purposes of education or for charitable purposes of any description. All such trust funds now held or subsequently received shall be administered with respect to investment and reinvestment, subject to any limitations in the trust, by the Commissioners of Finance. The City may also accept grants for its corporate purposes from any government, governmental agency or person.

4. CONDEMNATION -- Interest to be acquired. Whenever the City shall condemn any land for any public or municipal purpose, in all such cases the absolute and unqualified fee simple title to such land, or, when

the proceeding is in personam, all the right, title and interest of the owner or owners who are made parties to the proceeding, if they should not be the owners of the entire fee simple title, shall be condemned and acquired; so that neither the said land nor any interest therein, shall under any circumstances revert to the person or persons who shall be the owners thereof at the time of the condemnation, or who shall be parties to such proceeding in personam, nor to any person or persons claiming under him, her or them; provided, however, that when the condemnation shall be provided for by ordinance, the City may determine, and in the ordinance providing for the condemnation declare, that an interest, less than the fee simple interest, for a fixed and limited period of time, or some other limited interest, will suffice for the purpose or purposes for which the property is to be acquired, and under such circumstances, only such interest shall be condemned and acquired.

5. UNIFORM APPLICATION; HIGHWAYS. The Charter shall apply in every section of Baltimore City without distinction because of the date at which the same became a part of the city, and all existing streets, avenues, roads, alleys and bridges within the city, heretofore dedicated and accepted or condemned or otherwise established as roads or streets by any then proper public authority, are in all respects validly constituted public streets and highways of the City.

6. TAXES -- Uniformity. The taxes levied by the City, with respect to ownership of the same class of property or property rights, shall be uniform in rate throughout the entire city.

7. RECORDS -- Evidence, Disclosure. (a) A suitable record of all the proceedings, financial transactions and official acts of all municipal agencies, shall be kept, and a certified copy of said record, or any part thereof, under the corporate seal of the City shall be admissible in evidence in any court of this State as proof of such record, or such part thereof. Such record shall be available for public inspection unless otherwise expressly ordered by the head of the agency or the municipal officer by or on behalf of whom such record is kept; and in the event that written demand shall be made for the public disclosure of any matter deemed confidential by the head of such agency or by such municipal officer, such demand shall at once be referred to the Board of Estimates and said Board, after consultation with the City Solicitor as to the legal propriety of its action, may order the demanded disclosure to be made in whole or in part.

(b) The City may provide by ordinance for the making and keeping of all or some of such records on micro-film or by other method of reproduction and, when so made, for the destruction of the original records. Any such reproduction or print therefrom shall be in all respects the equivalent of the original from which made, and when authenticated as above provided shall be admissible in evidence in any court of this State as proof of such record, or such part thereof. . . .

(c) Unless otherwise directed by the Board of Estimates, every municipal agency of the City shall prepare annually a written report. . . .

BIBLIOGRAPHY

The works cited have been carefully selected to indicate the major sources to be consulted for further research on the growth of Baltimore. Materials listed have been published during the nineteenth and twentieth centuries. The variety of works was chosen in order to provide a cross-section of the information available on the social, economic, and political life of the city. Students should also consult Reader's Guide to Periodical Literature and Social Science and Humanities Index for additional articles on Baltimore.

PRIMARY SOURCES

An Act to Incorporate the Baltimore and Ohio Railroad Company. Passed at December Session, 1826. Baltimore, 1827.

Article Four, Public Laws (City of Baltimore) Containing the Charter of Baltimore City, and the Miscellaneous Local Laws, With any Additions Made by the General Assembly of 1927, . . ., Baltimore, 1927.

Baltimore. Records of the City. . ., 1729-1817. Baltimore, 1905-1909, 4 vols.

Baltimore. Reports of the City Officers and Departments, 1823-present.

Baltimore Board of Trade. Constitution and By-Laws, adopted 1849. Act of Incorporation passed by Maryland Assembly, May, 1852. Baltimore, 1878.

Baltimore Chamber of Commerce. Act of Incorporation and By-Laws as Amended of the Baltimore Corn and Flour Exchange. Adopted at a Meeting of the Board of Directors, January, 1856. Baltimore, 1860.

Baltimore, Maryland. Ordinances and Resolutions, 1827-present. Also for annual messages of the Mayor, 1827-1869.

Baltimore, Maryland. Trustees of Poor. By-Laws for the Government of the Poor, and Alms House of Baltimore City and County, 1826. Baltimore, 1826.

Baltimore, Maryland Council. Journal of the Proceedings of the First Branch of the City Council, 1828-1923.

──────────────── . Journal of the Proceedings of the Second Branch of the City Council, 1829-1923.

In 1923 the two branches of the council were abolished to form a council of one chamber. Then published under title: Journal of the Proceedings of the City Council, 1923-date.

Baltimore Reform League. Constitution and By-Laws. Baltimore, 1896.

Charter of Baltimore City. 1964 Revision, As Amended to January, 1969. Baltimore, 1969.

A Charter for the City of Baltimore Prepared by the Charter Board Elected at the General Election Held in the City of Baltimore on the Sixth Day of November, 1917. Baltimore, 1918.

The New Charter of Baltimore City, Enacted by the Acts of 1898, Ch. 123. With all Amendments and Addition Thereto Down to and Including the Acts of 1914. Baltimore, 1915.

Peabody Institute, Maryland. The Founder's Letters, and the Papers Relating to Its Dedication and Its History Up to the First January, 1868. Baltimore, 1868.

Proceedings of Sundry Citizens of Baltimore Convened for the Purpose of Devising the Most Efficient Means of Improving the Intercourse Between that City and the Western States, Baltimore, 1827. Proposal for building Baltimore and Ohio Railroad rather than a canal.

Report of the City Plan Committee of the City of Baltimore, Maryland on the Development of the Territory added under the Act of 1918, Together with Recommendations and Suggestions on the Railroad, Rapid Transit, and Harbor Problems of the City . . . . May 1, 1919. Baltimore, 1919.

Riordan, Michael Joseph. Cathedral Records From the Beginning of Catholicity in Baltimore to the Present Time. Baltimore, 1906.

SECONDARY SOURCES

Baltimore. Two Hundredth Anniversary, 1729-1929. Baltimore, 1929. Illustrates various aspects of the past as well as the attributes of the city in 1929.

The Baltimore American. Anniversary and Jubilee Edition. Baltimore, 1905. Discussion of paper's history and various industries of the time.

Baltimore Federation of Labor. Illustrated History of the Baltimore Federation of Labor and Its Affiliated Organizations. Baltimore, 1900.

Baltimore First National Bank. A Bank and Its Times, 1806-1956. Baltimore, 1956. Important for discussion of contributions of the bank.

Baltimore and Ohio Railroad Company. The Story of the Centenary Pageant of the Baltimore and Ohio Railroad Company, held at Baltimore, Maryland, Sept. 24 to Oct. 1927. Baltimore, 1927. Contains interesting sidelights and a historical sketch of the railroad.

Baltimore Savings Bank. The Savings Bank of Baltimore, One Hundred Years of Service, 1818-1918. Baltimore, 1918.

Beard, Gordon. Birds on the Wing; The Story of the Baltimore Orioles. Garden City, 1967. Fine discussion of the team and its relationships with the city.

Beirne, Francis F. The Amiable Baltimoreans. New York, 1952. Interesting history of the city.

Blum, Isidor. The Jews of Baltimore. Baltimore, 1910. Important discussion of contributions made in Baltimore.

Bond, Allen K. When the Hopkins Came to Baltimore. Baltimore, 1927. Fine explanation of the work of these important benefactors of the city.

Bornholdt, Laura. Baltimore and Early Pan-Americanism; A Study in the Background of the Monroe Doctrine. Northampton, Massachusetts, 1949.

Bready, James H. The Home Team, A Century of Baseball in Baltimore, 1859-1959; A Patriotic Story. Baltimore, 1958.

Brown, Alexander Crosby. Steam Packets on the Chesapeake; A History of the Old Bay Line Since 1840. Cambridge, Maryland, 1961.

Browne, W. H. George Calvert and Cecilius Calvert, Barons Baltimore of Baltimore. Baltimore, 1890. Good early study of the original proprietors.

Buchanan, William B. Baltimore: Or, Long, Long Time Ago. Baltimore, 1853. Poem, interesting for description.

Chapelle, Howard Irving. The Baltimore Clipper, Its Origins and Development. Hatboro, Pennsylvania, 1965. Important discussion of shipping industry and contributions of Baltimore shipbuilders.

Crooks, James B. Politics and Progress; The Rise of Urban Progressivism in Baltimore, 1895 to 1911. Baton Rouge, Louisiana, 1968. Examination of the Baltimore reform movement, comparing with similar ones in other American cities, placing it in the context of the national progressive movement.

Forrest, Clarence H. Official History of the Fire Department of the City of Baltimore, Together with Biographies and Portraits of Eminent Citizens. Baltimore, 1898.

Frey, Jacob. Reminiscences of Baltimore. Baltimore, 1893. Personal memories combined with historical data by a marshal of the police force.

Griffith, Thomas W. Annals of Baltimore. Baltimore, 1824. Important for detailed data of the city up to the date published.

Guilday, Doctor Peter. Life and Times of John Carrol, Archbishop of Baltimore. Baltimore, 1922. Thorough description of development and extension of the Catholic church in America.

Half-Century's Progress of the City of Baltimore. The City's Leading Manufacturers and Merchants. New York, 1886. Good description of territorial increase and population. Fine discussion of industries and leading manufacturers.

Hall, Clayton Colman, ed. Baltimore; Its History and Its People. New York, 1912, 3 vols. Fine history of various periods by different contributors in the first volume. Volumes 2 and 3 deal with specific institutions as well as sketches of distinguished citizens.

Hawkins, A. The Life and Times of Hon. Elijah Stansbury, an "Old Defender" and ex-Mayor of Baltimore; Together with Early Reminiscences Dating from 1662 and Embracing a Period of 212 Years. Baltimore, 1874. Discusses Stanbury's youth and his service to the city as mayor.

Hirschfeld, Charles. Baltimore, 1870-1900: Studies in Social History. Baltimore, 1941. Illustrates four aspects of the city, indicating changes in concepts and practices of education, growth of population, economic field, and development of industry and effects on labor.

Hollander, Jacob H. The Financial History of Baltimore. Baltimore, 1899.

Howard, George W. The Monumental City, Its Past History and Present Resources. Baltimore, 1873-1889.

Hungerford, Edward. The Story of the Baltimore and Ohio Railroad, 1827-1927. New York, 1927. Excellent story telling what the building of the line meant to the Atlantic Seaboard as well as the Mississippi Valley.

Janvier, Meredith. Baltimore in the Eighties and Nineties. Baltimore, 1933. Well told recollections and graphic pictures of life. Discusses the people he knew and grew up with through the early twentieth century.

────────────. Baltimore Yesterdays. Baltimore, 1937. Very good for glimpses of the life of youth and adults. Tells of Johns Hopkins University as well.

Latrobe, Ferdinand C. History of the Public Parks of Baltimore. Baltimore, 1896.

McKeldin, Theodore R. No Mean City. An Inquiry into Civic Greatness. Baltimore, 1964. Good description of how Baltimore has responded to the challenge of the postwar world.

Maryland, Commission on Interracial Problems and Relations. An American City in Transition; the Baltimore Community Self-Survey of Inter-group Relations. Baltimore, 1955. Discusses problems of races and how the city has been dealing with them.

Mencken, Henry, et. al. The Sunpapers of Baltimore. Written by four staff members. Includes much detail with interesting developments. Good addition to journalism.

Nelson, S. B., firm. History of Baltimore, Maryland, From its Founding as a Town to the Current Year, 1729-1898; Including its Early Settlement and Development; a Description of its Historic and Interesting Localities; Political, Military, Civil and Religious Statistics, Biographies of Representative Citizens. Baltimore, 1898.

Nicholls, Charles Wilbur de Lyon. Annals of a Remarkable Salon. Excerpts from My Johns Hopkins University Note Book. A Pen-Picture of Baltimore Society in 1876-80. New York, 1910.

Paine, Ralph D. Joshua Barney a Forgotten Hero of Blue Water. Baltimore, 1924. Rescues Barney from obscurity, a good addition to naval legends of the Revolution.

Powell, Lyman Pierson, ed. Historic Towns of the Southern States. New York, 1900. Brief description of the history and some major institutions of Baltimore.

Scharf, John Thomas. The Chronicles of Baltimore. Baltimore, 1874. Important contribution to history of the city, including detailed descriptions of its participation in the War of 1812 and the Civil War.

────────────. History of Baltimore City and County, from the Earliest Period to the Present Day: Including Biographical Sketches of Their Representative Men. Philadelphia, 1881. Important companion to his Chronicles.

────────────. The Natural and Industrial Resources and Advantages of Maryland, Being a Complete Description of all the Counties of the State, and the City of Baltimore. Annapolis, Maryland, 1892.

Semmes, Raphael. Baltimore as Seen By Visitors, 1783-1860. Baltimore, 1953. Interesting views of the city.

Silverman, Albert J., ed. Baltimore, City of Promise. (Produced by Senior High School Pupils of the Baltimore Public Schools.) Baltimore, 1953. Descriptions of various aspects of life in Baltimore.

Speer, Talbot Tyler. The Story of Baltimore Business Firms. New York, 1961.

Tuska, Benjamin. Know-Nothingism in Baltimore, 1854-1860. New York,

1925. Good description of the growth of the movement and its hold and influence on Baltimore.

Welsh, Lillian. Reminiscences of Thirty Years in Baltimore. Baltimore, 1925.

ARTICLES

"Baltimore's Centennial, 1829," from the American, Saturday, August 8, 1829, in Maryland Historical Magazine, vol. XXIV, 1929, 237 ff.

Benjamin, Marcus. "Maryland During the Revolution," Maryland Historical Magazine, vol. XXIV, 1929, 325 ff.

Bump, Charles Weathers. "The First Grants on the Patapsco," Maryland Historical Magazine, vol. III, 1908, 51 ff.

Gilmor, Robert. "Recollections of Baltimore," Maryland Historical Magazine, vol. VII, 1912, 233 ff.

Gordon, Douglas H. "Hero Worship as Expressed in Baltimore Street Names," Maryland Historical Magazine, vol. XXIII, 1948, 121 ff.

Leakin, George A., D.D. "Migrations of Baltimore Town," Maryland Historical Magazine, vol. I, 1906, 45 ff.

Steiner, B. C. "Maryland's Religious History," Maryland Historical Magazine, vol. XXI, 1926, 1 ff.

Wroth, Laurence C. "Poe's Baltimore," Johns Hopkins Alumni Magazine, vol. XVII, 1929, 299 ff.

NAME INDEX

Abbott, Horace, 36
Abbott, Mr., 43
Adams, Alvin, 39
Adams, President John, 21
Adams, President John Quincy, 29, 31
Adams, Joseph, 4
Agnew, Governor Spiro, 84, 85
Albaugh, John W., 64
Allen, John W., 18
Allen, Zacahariah, 12
Amrein, Ralph, 82
Anderson, James, 56
Angus, Gen. Felix, 71
Archibald, Commissioner, 6
Astor, John Jacob, 12
Asburym, Francis, 7

Bagley, Rt. Rev. James Roosevelt, Archbishop, 56
Baker, George, 41
Ball, James, 28
Baltimore, Lord, 1
Banks, General, 50
Banks, Mayor Robert T., 54
Barnet, Major, 12
Barnetz, Daniel, 4
Barnetz, Leonard, 4
Barney, Joshua, 9, 14, 16
Barney, Mrs. Mary, 33
Barnum, D., 30
Barnum, P.T., 40
Barye, M., 61
Bayard, Senator, 56
Bayley, John, 3
Beach, J.J., 34
Bell, John, 49
Bentley, Mrs. Helen Delich, 85
Blackhawk, Indian Chief, 34
Blair, John, 16
Bombaugh, C.C., 52
Bonaparte, Charles, 59
Bonaparte, Elizabeth Patterson, 25
Bonaparte, Jerome, 22, 25, 59
Bonaparte, Napoleon, 22
Bond, H. Lennox, 56
Borady, Mayor Samuel, 38
Bowley, Daniel, 12
Braddock, General, 5
Bradford, Governor, 51
Breckinridge, John C., 49
Broening, Mayor W.F., 74, 76
Bronson, Joseph, 35
Brown, Alexander, 24
Brown, B. Gratz, 56
Brown, Mayor George William, 49, 50
Brown, John, 6
Brundage, Avery, 79
Brune, John C., 50

Bryan, William Jennings, 73
Buchanan, Andrew, 8, 15
Buchanan, Dr. George, 3
Buchanan, James, 23
Buchanan, William, 5, 17
Bucher, Lieutenant, 82
Buckler, William H., 69
Buckner, William, 3
Butler, Gen. William O., 42

Calhoun, Mayor James, 20
Calvert, Caroline, 7
Carey, Dr. M., 76
Carlile, John, 17
Carnegie, Andrew, 71
Carroll, Charles, 2, 3
Carroll, Charles, Jr., 5
Carroll, Charles, 31, 32, 34
Carroll, Daniel, 2, 3
Carroll, David H., 69
Carroll, James, 17
Carroll, Rt. Rev. John, Bishop, 16, 17, 21, 26
Carter, Edward F., 50
Carter, Police Marshal, 74
Cass, Gen. Lewis, 42
Caton, Mr., 16
Chapman, Mayor John Lee, 50
Chase, George, 17
Chase, Samuel, 15, 19
Cheatham, Jon, 28
Chequier, Charles, 17
Christie, James, Jr., 9
Clark, Mr. 35
Clarke, Abraham, 1
Clay, Henry, 33, 40
Claypoole, Captain, 42
Cloud, Charles F., 33, 36, 38, 46
Cloud, R.M., 38, 46
Coale, William R., 51
Cocke, Dr., 23
Cohen, B.I., 34
Cole, Thomas, 1, 19, 21
Collett, John, 1
Coltin, Dr., 40
Columbus, Christopher, 65
Comegys, John, 23
Cook, Jay, 22
Cooper, Peter, 32, 36
Copely, Governor, 2
Cornwallis, General, 10, 11
Cox, Melville B., 31
Cruse, Peter, 28

D'Alesandro, Thomas, Jr., 81, 82; Mayor, 83, 84, 85
Dallas, George M., 40
Davidge, Dr., 23
Davidson, Robert C., 63
Davies, Jacob G., 40
Davis, John W., 50

Dinsmore, W.B., 39
Dix, Gen. John A., 51
Dobbin, George W., 50
Dobbin, Thomas, 18
Donaldson, John J., 39
Donelson, Andrew Jackson, 46
Douglas, Stephen A., 49
Duffy, Edward, 60
Dulany, W.C., 33
Dunbar, Dr., 37
Duncan, John, 28
Durang, Charles, 25

Eaton, Jeremiah, 2
Eccleston, Archbishop, 44
Eden, Mrs. Caroline Calvert, 7
Eden, Governor Robert, 7
Edwards, Major, 13
Edwards, Phillip, 18
Ellicott, John, 17
Ellicott, Mr., 34
Elliot, Thomas, 12, 19
Ellmakeer, Amos, 33
Essy, Edwards, Esq., 22
Evans, Oliver, 15
Everett, Edward, 49

Fell, Edward, 3, 6
Fillmore, Millard, 46
Fite, Jacob, 10
Fitzpatrick, Senator, 49
Fitz-roy, Mr., 84
Flanigan, Mr., 25
Ford, John T., 47
Frazier, Capt. David, 4
Freylinghuysen, Theodore, 40
Fuller, E.F., 69

Gaither, C.D., 86
Garland, H.M., 42, 43
Garrett, Miss Mary, 63
Gart, Mr., 13
Gatchell, William, 50
Gay, Nicholas R., 6
Gibbons, Archbishop James, 62; Cardinal, 70, 73
Giles, Judge, 55
Gilman, Dr. Daniel Coit, 58, 69
Gilmor, Robert, 17, 23, 28, 29
Gipson, William, 19
Gist, Brig. Gen. Mordecai, 13
Gist, Richard, 3
Glenn, John, 63
Goddard, William, 9
Goldsmith, William C., 22
Gorsuch, Charles, 1
Gorsuch, John, 1
Goodwin, Lyde, 15
Goucher, Dr., 63
Gough, Harry Dorsey, 8, 14
Grady, J.H., 83

153

154 BALTIMORE

Graham, David, 17
Graham, William A., 45
Grandchut, Mr., 5
Grant, Daniel, 15
Grant, Gen. Ulysses S., 52
de Grasse, Count, 10
Gray, Judge J.B., Jr., 81
Greely, First Lieutenant, 59
Greely, Horace, 56
Greene, Maj. Gen. Nathaniel, 10, 12, 13
Griest, Isaac, 8
Griffith, Benjamin, 6, 8
Griffith, Isaac, 8
Grover, George O., 51
Gwinn, Charles, 25

Hale, Capt. Philip M., 41
Hall, Thomas, 47, 50
Hallam, Mr., 15
Hamilton, William, 3
Hammond, Col. William, 3
Hand, Adjutant General, 11
Hanson, Mayor John, 43
Hanson, Jonathan, 2, 7
Harding, President Warren G., 76
Harper, Robert G., 26
Harris, J. Morrison, 37
Harrison, Benjamin, 9
Harrison, William Henry, 38
Hart, Jacob, 17
Hayes, Mayor Thomas, 68
Hays, John, 12
Heener, Meecher, 5
Heiskell, J. Monroe, 60, 61
Henderson, Robert, 12
Henry, Mr., 15
Hermange, E.V., 56
Heuisler, Charles W., 69
Heuisler, William J., 39
Hewes, Mr., 22
Hicks, Governor, 50
Higginbotham, Ralph, 22
Hillen, Mayor Solomon, Jr., 39
Hinks, Charles D., 50
Hinks, Samuel, 46
Hodges, Mayor James, 61
Hoffman, D., 26
Hollingsworth, Jesse, 7, 8
Holmes, John, 7
Hooper, Mayor Alcaeus, 64, 67
Hopkins, Johns, 39, 56, 57
Houston, Gen. Samuel, 41
Howard, Charles, 50
Howard, John Edgar, 4
Howard, Col. John Eager, 30
Howell, Capt. Thomas, 1
Howland, Daniel, 19, 27
Hull, Thomas M., 47
Hull, Thomas V., Jr., 50
Hunt, Mayor Jesse, 34, 35, 36, 42

Hyrne, Major, 13

Jackson, Gen. Andrew, 28, 33; President, 34
Jackson, Mayor Howard W., 76, 77, 79, 80, 81
Jencks, Francis M., 69
Jenkins, Michael, 71
Jessop, Charles, 17
Jessop, William, 17, 22
Job, Mr., 25
Johnson, President Andrew, 51, 53
Johnson, Dr. Edward, 16
Johnson, Mayor Edward, 23, 28, 29
Johnson, Herschel V., 49
Johnson, James, 17
Johnson, President Lyndon B., 84
Johnson, Richard M., 35
Jones, Phillip, 3
Jones, William F., 35

Kane, Mayor George P., 50, 58
Kayser, William, 69
Kell, Thomas, 26
Kellogg, Mr., 35
Kelly, Capt. Matthew, 41
Kemp, Dr. James, Bishop, 26
Kennedy, John P., 28
Kenney, S.P., 36
Kenrick, Archbishop Francis Patrick, 51
Kent, Emanuel, 21
Kerr, Charles J., 47
Key, Francis Scott, 25, 73
Keyser, Samuel, 69
King, William R., 44
Kossuth, Louis, 44

Lafayette, Marquis de, 11, 14, 29
Lafollette, Senator Robert M., 76
La Lanne, Amie de, 10
Land, Joseph, 49
Latrobe, Mayor Ferdinand C., 57, 58, 60, 61, 65, 66, 73
Latrobe, John H.B., 57
Lawson, W.P., 80
Leakin, Mayor Sheppard C., 37
Lee, Governor Thomas Sim, 12
Lee, Mrs. Thomas Sim, 12
Lee, Richard Henry, 9
Leggett, George, 17
Legum, J., 75
Len, Mr., 41
Leo XIII, Pope, 70
Leucht, Joseph, 53
Leypold, Mr., 13
Lincoln, President Abraham, 49, 50, 51, 52
Lind, Jenny, 43
Lipp, F.K., 44
Little, Mr., 7
Littlejohn, Dr. M., 21

Long, Robert, 17
Lowe, Governor, 44
Lowndes, Governor, 67, 68
Lucas, Edmund, 35
Lux, George, 14
Lux, William, 8
Lyford, William G., 37
Lyon, William, 6
Lytle, Mr., 5

Macaulay, Patrick, 36
McCausland, Marcus, 21
McColgan, Reverend, 39
McCrea, S., 21
MacCrery, William, 21
McDonald, Michael, 41
McDonald, William, 25
McElderry, Thomas, 22
McHenry, Col. James, 18, 24
Mackay, Clifford W., 85
Mackeimer, Captain, 15
McKeldin, Governor Theodore R., 81, 83, Mayor, 84
Mackie, Ebenezer, 16
McKenzie, Dr., 23
McKim, Alexander, Jr., 22
McKim, Isaac, 26
McLane, Isaac, 26
McLane, Mayor Robert, 70, 71
Maddox, Miss Ella H., 69
Mahool, Mayor J. Barry, 72
Malster, William T., 67
Mankin, Henry, 43
Mann, Mr. 13
Marburg, Charles, 73
Marechal, Rev. Ambrose, 27; Archbishop, 31
Marshall, Chief Justice John, 35
Marshall, Thomas, 35
Martin, Alexander, 21, 22
Mary, Queen, 2
Mason, Capt. William, 41
Mayer, Mr. Brantz, 42
Mayers, Jacob, 5
Meredith, Jonathan, 26
Miles, Clarence W., 82
Miller, A., 79
Minckler, W.M., 53
Moale, John, 6, 8, 10, 15
Moale, Richard, 8
Moale, Richard H., 19
Montgomery, Mayor Jon, 28, 29
Montross, Thomas, 1
Moranville, Rev. John Francis, 26
Morgan, B.M., 76
Morse, Samuel F.B., 40, 41
Mosler, Col. James, 29
Mountenay, Alexander, 1
Murdoch, Mr., 54
Murdock, William, 6
Murphy, John, 38

NAME INDEX

Murphy, John, 64
Murphy, William, 13

Neale, Rev. Leonard, Bishop, 27
Neilson, William H., 50
Nelson, Benjamin, 6
Newcomer, Benjamin F., 68
Nice, Governor, 80
Nicholson, Benjamin, 17
Nicholson, Judge, 25
Niles, Hezekiah, 24
Niles, William Ogden, 24, 38
Nixon, Vice President Richard M., 82
Norris, J. Cloud, 51

O'Donnell, John, 14, 17
Oliver, John, 26, 29
Owens, H., 77
Owens, J.W., 80

Pace, William, 16
Patten, George, 7
Patterson, Miss Elizabeth, 22
Patterson, William, 12, 16, 22, 26
Payson, Henry, 22, 26, 27
Peabody, George, 47
Peale, Rembrandt, 24, 25
Pechin, Mr., 19
Pendleton, Edmond, 9
Pennington, Josiah, 28
Perkins, Captain, 8
Perry, Com. Stephen, 25
Peters, George A., 35
Peters, Thomas, 13
Peters, W.C., 43
Phelps, Charles E., 60
Philips, J., Jr., 30
Pierce, Gen. Franklin, 44
Pinckney, William, 29
Pinkney, William, 59
Poe, Edgar Allan, 43, 57, 72, 76
Polk, President James K., 40, 41
Poppleton, Mr. T., 29
Porter, David, 19, 20
Poultney, Evan, 31, 35
Powder, Mr., 36
Pratt, Enoch, 59, 65, 68
Prentiss, Mr., 21
Preston, Mayor James H., 73, 74
Priestley, James, 21
Pulaski, Count, 10
Purviance, Samuel, 6, 8, 12

Randall, Aquilla, 27
Randall, Joseph K., 42
Raine, Samuel, 17
Raine, William, 39
Raines, Frederick, 38, 45
Randolph, Peyton, 9
Raynor, William, 57
Reeder, Charles, 35

Reinagle, Mr., 18
Remsen, Ira, 69
Ridgely, Richard, 12
Rigson, Alexander, 17
Rinehart, Mr., 64
Ringgold, Thomas, 6
Robinson, George, 8
Robinson, Joseph, 47
Rochambeau, Maj. Gen. Count de, 11, 12
Rockefeller, John D., Jr., 70
Rogers, Mr., 40
Rogers, Philip, 20
Roosevelt, Theodore, 73
Rushworth, Richard, 28
Russell, Thomas, 12
Russell, William, 15
Rutter, Thomas, 22

Sands, Mr., 41
Sanford, Edward S., 39
Schnauffer, Charles Henry, 44
Schneck, Maj. Gen. Robert C., 51
Scott, Gen. Winfield, 45
Sergent, John, 33
Sharpe, Governor Horatio, 5, 7
Sheeco, Dr., 23
Sherry, Police Lieutenant, 82
Sherwood, Arthur, 84
Shipley, W., 30
Shirk, Henry, 61
Shoemaker, Samuel, 39
Short, Joseph H., Jr., 82
Skillman, Charles, 35
Skinner, John S., 32, 43
Sless, L.B., 75
Small, Mayor Jacob, 30
Smallwood, Major General, 13
Smith, Campbell, 17
Smith, Dennis A., 26
Smith, Gen. J. Spear, 39
Smith, Dr. James, 21
Smith, John, 5, 7
Smith, Mayor John, 45
Smith, Major General, 18, 24
Smith, Robert, 28
Smith, Samuel, 12
Smith, Gen. Samuel, 36
Smith, Mayor Thorowgood, 19, 22
Smith, William, 8, 9
Smyth, Dr., 23
Sower, Mr., 22
Spaulding, Archbishop Martin J., 52, 55
Spear, William, 6
Spencer, Herbert, 60
Squires, Captain, 9
Steretts, John, 12, 13
Sterrit, James, 5, 10
Steiger, Mr., 8, 10
Steiger, Andrew, 4

Stevenson, Dr. Henry, 4, 5
Stevenson, Dr. John, 4, 14
Stewart, Richardson, 21
Stewart, Robert, 22
Stewart, William B., 60
Stewart, Mayor William, 29, 33
Stiles, Mayor George, 27, 28
Stockett, Henry, 1
Stockett, Capt. Thomas, 1
Stodder, David, 20
Striker, John, 17
Stump, John, 17
Swann, Mayor Thomas, 46, 48, 49
Sweezym Warden, 76
Swift, General, 31

Taft, President William H., 73
Taney, Roger B., Chief Justice, 44
Tawes, Governor, 84
Taylor, John, 1
Taylor, William, 21
Taylor, Gen. Zachary, 41
Tennant, Thomas, 26
Teny, A.G., 36
Thomas, Evan, 30
Thomas, Philip E., 30
Thompson, Henry, 26
Thompson, Mr., 19
Tilghman, Edward, 6
Timanus, Mayor E. Clay, 71, 72
Todd, James, 2
Tolley, Maj. Thomas, 3
Townsend, A. McKim, 16
Travers, William H., 48
Treadway, John, 17
Truman, President Harry S., 82
Truxton, Capt, Thomas, 20
Turnbull, Mr., 54
Twining, Nathaniel, 11
Tyson, Elisha, 17, 21
Tyson, Philip, 51

Ulman, A.J., 69

Vanbibber, Mr., 16
Van Buren, President Martin, 33, 35, 38
Vanhorne, Gabriel, 11
Vansant, Joshua, 55

Wagner, Jacob, 23
Walker, Dr. George, 3
Walker, Mr., 19
Walmsley, Rev. Charles, Bishop of Rama, 11
Walters, William T., 61
Warner, Thomas, 24
Washington, George, General and President, 9, 10, 11, 13, 16, 17, 19, 23
Washington, Martha, 11

Watson, M.S., 81
Webb, G.W., 39
Weischampel, J.F, Sr., 34
Welch, John, 28
Wells, George, 8, 9
Wesley, John, 7
Wetson, John, 17
White, Rev. Charles J., 38
White, Capt. Joseph, 14
White, Julian Le Roy, 69
Whitfield, Archbishop James, 35
Wigman, H., 38

Wignell, Mr., 18
Wilde, Oscar, 60
Wildey, Thomas, 28
William, King, 2
Williams, Otto H., 15
Williams, General, 17
Williams, Mr., 19
Wilman, Mr., 33
Wilmer, Mr., 19
Wilson, Stephen, 17
Wilson, Thomas, 26
Winans, Mrs. Thomas, 47

Winchester, David, 23
Winchester, George, 31
Winchester, William, 22
Wirt, William, Postmaster General, 32, 33
Wood, James H., 34
Woodward, John, 8
Wool, Gen. John E., 51
Wright, Richard, 7
Wright, Silas M., 40
Wyman, William, 69

Yeo, Rev. John, 2